The Plaza, First and Always

by William S Worley

Foreword by Miller Nichols

ADDAX
PUBLISHING
GROUP

Bob Snodgrass
Publisher

Gary Carson
Photo Editor

Gib Twyman
Managing Editor

Brad Breon
Publishing Consultant

Darcie Kidson
Publicity

Randy Breeden
Art Direction/Design

Dust jacket design by Jerry Hirt

Dust jacket photos by Gary Carson

Production Assistance: Michelle Washington, Sharon Snodgrass, David Power, Jeremy Styno

Select Photos Courtesy of the J.C. Nichols Company, the Plaza Merchants Association, Lightfoot Photography, High View Aerial Photography

Published by Addax Publishing Group, 8643 Hauser Drive, Suite 235 Lenexa, Kansas 66215

Printed and bound in Canada

DISTRIBUTED TO THE TRADE BY ANDREWS AND MCMEEL, 4520 Main Street, Kansas City, Missouri 64111-7701

ISBN: 1-886110-25-5 (Collectors Edition, Leather)
ISBN: 1-886110-19-0 (General Edition, Hardback)

Library of Congress Cataloging-in-Publication Data

Worley, William S.
    The Plaza, first and always / by William S. Worley.
       p.   cm.
      ISBN 1-886110-25-5 (alk. paper)
      1. Country Club Plaza (Shopping center : Kansas City, Mo.)
    2. Shopping centers—Missouri—Kansas City. I. Title.
    HF5430.5.K2W67 1997
    381'.1'09778411—dc21   97-18963
                                                                 CIP

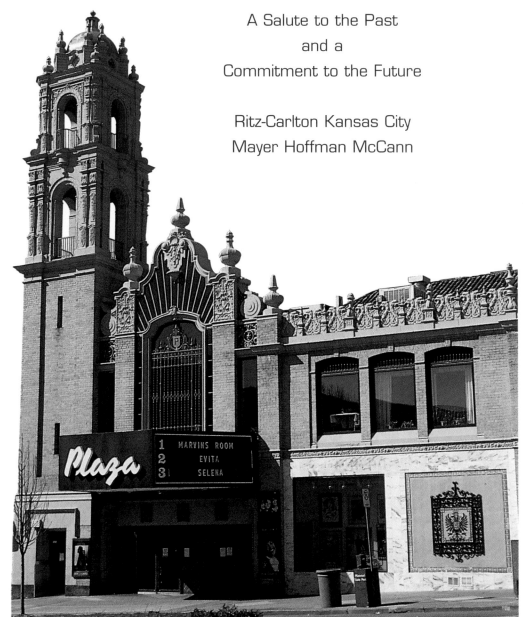

A Salute to the Past
and a
Commitment to the Future

Ritz-Carlton Kansas City
Mayer Hoffman McCann

The Plaza, First and Always

Table of Contents

The Plaza, First and Always

Acknowledgements

This book would not have been possible without the assistance of many individuals. Great thanks go to Barbara Barickman at the J.C. Nichols Co. for arranging interviews and making historic photos available. Thanks as well go to many current and past J.C. Nichols Company employees who agreed to talk with me about their labors of love.

Photo Editor Gary Carson proved to be much more than just a "picture man." His interest in the project and creative genius provided much stimulation and many beautiful scenes for readers to enjoy.

Editor Gib Twyman performed yeoman duty in helping turn often turgid prose into much more clear English. We may not always agree on commas and hyphens, but his suggested word choice was unerring.

Revisiting the historical materials concerning the Plaza was made easier by David, Jennifer, Betty, and Marilyn, the staff at Western Historical Manuscripts Collection, repository of the J.C. Nichols Company Scrapbooks and Collection.

Sources of information for the text came from interviews by the author with persons cited and from the J.C. Nichols Company scrapbooks. The latter are available for public use at the Western Historical Manuscript Collection, University of Missouri-Kansas City.

Here's to the Plaza! May it serve as Kansas City's second Downtown throughout the 21st Century and beyond!

Bill Worley

Hyde Park, Kansas City, Mo.

Foreword

The Plaza is a Kansas City crown jewel.

There are many beautiful places in our town, wonderful and special in their own way, but I have been told that nothing so touches a chord or evokes the fond feelings of Kansas Citians, and nothing charms visitors, like The Plaza.

For hundreds, more likely thousands, of our citizenry birthdays anniversaries, romantic meals and evening strolls are images that emerge when we think of The Plaza...along with Easter bunnies, Art Fairs, and the Christmas lights. We hold these memories dear.

I believe that is why so many have come to think of it as our Plaza, as well as The Plaza. Whether a person lives in Kansas City, Olathe, Liberty, Lee's Summit or any of the surrounding communities, there is a sense of "ownership" when we speak of The Plaza.

As changes occur which are perceived to threaten the character, nature or well-being to The Plaza, people react. Even if they live in outlying areas and don't visit that often, people still want to know: "What's new on the Plaza? What's coming to the Plaza?" They feel a kinship and a loyalty often reserved for sports teams and personal affiliations.

Some of that, I don't think is by accident. Some of it was accidental ... or our good fortune. From the very first, The Plaza was never planned to be "just a place to shop." It was designed to be unique, with one distinct harmonious architectural flavor - Spanish Mediterranean. Conceived as the first large-scale shopping center in America accommodating the automobile, it was designed as a place, not just welcoming, but celebrating the family ... early on with a pony ring and Tom Thumb miniature golf.

Much of what we know today evolved quite naturally from the fact that the Plaza became the abiding passion and vision of one family. For the head of that family, my father, J.C. Nichols, The Plaza became the heart and center of his business and personal endeavors. From its inception in 1922, the J.C. Nichols Company, led by my father until 1950, deliberately and carefully developed The Plaza as a shopping center made profitable by its unique amenities and as a gathering place for residents and visitors to this city.

When the leadership mantel was passed to me, I strived to carry on The Plaza tradition in the spirit my father started and to extend it, wherever possible. Replacing the former filling stations with garden courtyards, introducing shops and stores of national prestige during the 1980's, beautifying with sculpture, flowers, lighting...

And so today The Plaza continues as a special urban place which has become a geographical center for the metropolitan area. And at a time when many people don't walk or stroll urban America, people do this every day and evening of the year on The Plaza. They do it not only with a sense of safety and freedom, but also enjoying the style and grace of its architecture and its welcoming ambiance.

To me that seems fitting because for decades The Plaza has touched important moments for so many of us. That is what *The Plaza, First and Always*, is intended to convey in its perceptive text and enticing photographs. The message is simple: from the J.C. Nichols Company family, to your family, and for all those who come here in the future, The Plaza will strive to remain close to the heart of Kansas City.

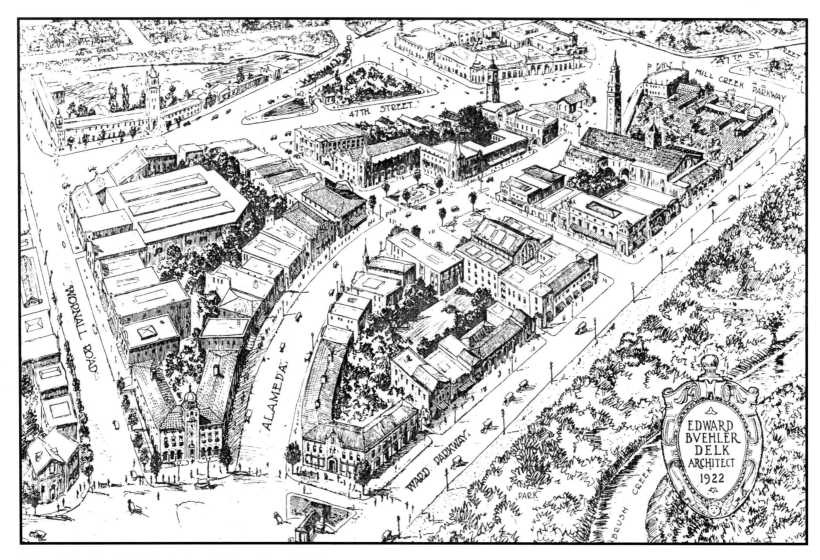

Edward Buehler Delk Rendering of Plaza Plan, 1922.

Herbert Hare designed the land plan for the Country Club Plaza in consultation with George Kessler. Delk came to Kansas City in 1919 at Nichols' invitation to apply his architectural skills. Because the first publicity of the Plaza plan was designed to convey more of the architectural detail than of the land design, Delk did the rendering rather than Hare or one of his draftsmen. Note that Alameda [Nichols] Road originally followed an "S" curve from the intersection of Mill Creek [J.C. Nichols] Parkway & 47th Street to Broadway & Ward Parkway. Hare and Nichols later adjusted Alameda Road to become an angled east-west route so that more regular building sizes could be accommodated.

Chapter 1:
Before the Plaza Was the Plaza

ORIGINALLY, KANSAS City had little in the way of urban planning to distinguish it from dozens of other river towns in the United States. Its 1838 town site map displayed streets running either parallel with or perpendicular to the Missouri River landing point.

By the time it incorporated in 1850, landowners made it clear they wanted their lots and subdivisions surveyed "square with the world." By that they meant square with the compass. Thus, today's River Market area of Kansas City, Missouri, is slightly out of kilter with the rest of the city. Aside from that small redirection, land speculators were quite content to let the city grow as it would.

What resulted was the standard gridiron of streets, unrelieved by variation or much greenery. In the 1880s, as the city outgrew itself twice in the decade, preachers and publishers called for some urban improvements. Using Chicago as an example, Kansas City leaders wanted parks and boulevards for their city, too.

Until the booming 1880s, there had been little need to think about parks because enough vacant land was scattered about, even in the middle of town, to keep folks distracted. As Kansas City jumped from 55,000 to 132,000 residents in just 10 years, new construction took most of the vacant lots. Open space became scarce.

The city had never been a green haven. Dirt in dry weather and mud in the wet seasons were the order of the day. A few hardy souls planted trees, bushes and flowers, usually only to have them chewed up by neighboring horses or other livestock. Minister Harry Hopkins of the First Congregational Church and Publisher William Rockhill Nelson of the *Kansas City Star* called for parks to become the "lungs of the city."

Boulevards were intended to connect the park sites and to provide something of a park-like environment along their edges. In a city where almost no street trees existed, the idea of planting anywhere from two to four rows of trees along roadways seemed almost revolutionary.

Two gentlemen heard the call particularly. August Meyer was a wealthy industrialist, born in St. Louis to immigrant parents, who owned and managed a metal smelter in the community of Argentine, Kan. Meyer let it be known in the early 1890s that he would be willing to put some of his engineering expertise to work helping create parks and boulevards.

The second major player, and certainly the one who remained involved longer, George Kessler, was a German immigrant, raised in Dallas, Texas,

The First Fountain on the Plaza.

Chandler's Nursery and Floral constructed its first building on land purchased from J.C. Nichols in 1916. The structure seen in the background reflects a substantial remodeling accomplished according to the design of young Nichols Company architect Edward Tanner. Nichols placed this first fountain at the intersection of 47th Street and Mill Creek [J.C. Nichols] Parkway in 1924.

Suydam [Mill Creek] Building, Sinclair Gasoline Station, and Wolferman Building [under construction].

The Nichols Company completed the Suydam Building as the first structure built after the announcement of the 1922 Plaza plan. Named for the largest of its first six tenants, Suydam Decorating Company, the building went up according to a Delk design. It won the 1924 Architect's League award for the best designed building constructed in Kansas City during 1923. The Sinclair station actually opened before any tenants moved into the Suydam. Wolferman's grocery was built by the Nichols Company for Fred Wolferman who insisted on owning his own structure. By the 1990s when Commerce Bank owned it, this building was only one of two on the entire Plaza not owned by the J.C. Nichols Company.

and educated in his home country. He came to Kansas City in 1882 to work for the Kansas City, Ft. Scott and Memphis Railroad. His job was to landscape around the line's new stations and to superintend a southeastern Kansas catalpa tree plantation, maintained for producing railroad ties.

After a number of false starts, Meyer succeeded in becoming president of the second Parks Board appointed in Kansas City. In 1892, Kessler agreed to serve as paid secretary and unpaid engineer to the Board of Parks and Boulevards. Within five years, the Board had a plan. It commenced park and street land acquisition and received a bountiful gift in the form of

Swope Park. By 1905, the construction of Independence Boulevard was complete, and construction moved apace on Meyer and Kessler's center-piece—a beautified and widened roadway they called The Paseo after the well-known boulevard in Mexico City—El Paseo de la Reforma.

In that same year of 1905, twenty-five-year-old Jesse Clyde Nichols convinced his real estate partners in Kansas City and some farmer friends near his hometown, Olathe, to invest in some raw land south of Brush Creek and the then Kansas City limits. Since 1904, Nichols had engaged in the real estate business with his partners, the brothers Reed. They initially bought land, built inexpensive houses (total cost: $900.00 for house

Battery Room in Barker's Garage Behind Suydam Building.

In the middle 1920s automobile batteries had to be charged regularly. The Barker Garage served both merchants on the Plaza and tenants in nearby apartment buildings with their own cars. Possibly the most stylish garage in the city upon completion, Edward Buehler Delk added exterior decorations to disguise the mundane use of the interior. This building survives in the 1990s as part of a parking garage for Commerce Bank.

and lot) in the Quindaro section of Kansas City, Kan. The move to more expensive land on the Missouri side required Nichols to increase his basic house prices from around $1,000 each to a minimum of $2,500 for house and lot.

Nichols envisioned a totally planned neighborhood, and by 1908, that vision included ownership or control of marketing for more than 1,000 acres of land adjoining the southern boundary of Kansas City, Mo., at that time. Nichols consulted with George Kessler, who had been hired by landowner Hugh Ward, on the layout of a boulevard through part of the property he planned to sell.

In 1911, Nichols watched as a competing realtor with a more conven-

Aerial view of the Plaza, 1931.

Between 1927 and 1930, the McCandless Company constructed the five high-rise apartment buildings lining Brush Creek. The Nichols Company arranged for construction of the Walnuts during the same period. This exclusive cooperative apartment immediately became one of the most exclusive addresses in all of Kansas City.

In this photo, the Walnuts stand in the foreground, with the rear of the Brush Creek structures lying to the north toward the developing Plaza at the top of the picture.

tional vision, subdivided a small area at the very beginning of today's Ward Parkway. That was the name Nichols and Vassie James Ward, widow of Hugh Ward, used for the roadway Kessler planned to honor Hugh Ward who died in 1909.

The competing realtor, George Law, named his subdivision "Country Club Plaza." He subdivided the lots into narrow 25- and 40- foot widths, intending to sell them to working people and buyers responding to his mail order ads in newspapers across the U.S. The lots sold better to out-of-towners because locals knew they had no protection from spring floods or summer rains which frequently caused flash flooding. Law apparently did not worry that the term "plaza" meant "marketplace" in its original Spanish context; he simply capi-

Plaza Theater, interior of stage, 1928

The Spanish theme carried on throughout the interior of the ornate Plaza Theater when it opened. The decorative detail rivaled that in its contemporary, the Midland, in Downtown Kansas City. The first "talkies" appeared at the same time so the theater featured acoustics to enhance the newly required sound equipment.

With the opening of the Plaza Theater, area residents began to see the entire Plaza area as an entertainment destination as well as a shopping spectacular.

Architect's Conception of the First Site Planned for the Giralda Tower. 1929

Drawn by Nichols' future son-in-law, this plan never worked out. Nichols and others judged the tower too massive for the site at Alameda [Nichols] Rd. and Broadway. Currently the site of Helzberg's Diamonds, this corner remained unbuilt until the late 1940s.

Giralda Tower, Seville Cathedral, Seville, Spain, 1965

The original tower in the southern Spanish city stands twice as tall as its smaller twin constructed on the Plaza. Constructed in the 14th century, the Seville version featured an interior ramp to the top allowing mounted riders quickly to ascend to the bell tower to view possible enemy attack. A careful examination of the lower left area of the photo reveals the location of the original Seville Light, a copy of which stands across 47th Street from the Plaza Tower.

Robert Whitmer of the Nichols Company and Sr. Arturo Castelanz, a Spanish Journalist inspect plans for the soon-to-completed Giralda Tower. 1967.

Bob Whitmer served as the Nichols Company's chief of public relations for more than two decades. One of his most strenuous efforts surrounded the planning, construction and opening of the new symbol of the Plaza. In this photo, he described the construction process to the visiting Spanish journalist. Completed in October, 1967, the Tower initially served as the focal point for the new Swanson's store building [Mark Shale and Cheesecake Factory].

talized on the attraction created by the name "Country Club."

In 1914, as war clouds gathered over the Balkans in southeastern Europe, Nichols and one of his salesmen quietly began buying up the lots scattered about by Law's mail-order sales barrage. George Tourtellot became the primary buyer of land for what became the Country Club Plaza shopping center.

Nichols' interest in developing shopping centers came from his early experience in selling house-building lots in this then-outlying section. Refrigeration was almost unknown; iceboxes kept food edible for short periods, but regular store visits by women were necessary for food supplies if nothing else.

Not many women were excited by the prospect of living far from grocery stores and meat markets. The distance meant they would have to ride a somewhat unpredictable trolley car for 10 or 15 minutes one-way each time they needed to shop. From this, Nichols realized that women were critical parts of the home-selling equation. He also learned that proximity to shopping was a high priority for these women.

Nichols' first effort in this direction was stopgap to say the least. At 51st Street and Brookside he constructed a two-store block in which one of the tenants always needed to be a grocery dealer. By the time he directed George Tourtellot to buy lots in the Country Club Plaza subdivision, Nichols already planned another shopping center at 63rd and Brookside. The Great War interrupted these plans; Brookside Center did not open until 1919.

Clearly, the primary reason behind the shopping centers in Nichols' mind was to increase convenience for the women in the families he hoped to attract to his new residential area—the Country Club District. He successfully convinced the Parks Board to include Brookside in the expanded system of beautified roadways criss-crossing his developments. Thus, one of the most singular planning activities in Kansas City history combined with the marketing skills of J.C. Nichols to create a complete

home-and-shop environment around the edges of the District.

Ever careful to place his activities in the path of progress, Nichols lobbied and gained approval for a boulevard from the old Westport community down to Brush Creek, the northern border for much of his development activity. As noted, he worked with Kessler and Vassie Ward to connect Ward Parkway with this boulevard connection to Westport known as Mill Creek Parkway. Then, just as he had successfully lobbied the Metropolitan Street Railway Company to buy up an old steam suburban railroad to Dodson (85th & Prospect) and turn it into the electrified "Country Club Line," Nichols also got the city to build and maintain Brookside Boulevard on the east side of this land.

Before some latter day anti-tax fanatic starts crying "foul!" it must be pointed out that Nichols either donated or arranged for donation of the land for Ward Parkway, Brookside and Meyer Boulevards. In most other areas of the city, boulevard and park areas had to be purchased. Sometimes court proceedings were necessary to complete the purchase. Thus, it was most helpful to the city and the Park Board that Nichols and his financial backers gave the land without condemnation proceedings.

Initially, Ward Parkway ran only on the north side of Brush Creek and on the west side of the wide park area presently encompassed by the roadway. The creek itself mostly followed its own meandering path through the valley. Over time, in some spots, Nichols or others put up stone embankments to direct the channel. Until the 1930s, however, Brush Creek had the normal dirt and gravel bed of any suburban stream.

As George Tourtellot's land acquisition efforts came to fruition, a few things appeared on the future shopping site. Chandler's Floral moved its showroom to a site at the junction of Mill Creek and Ward Parkways in 1916. Then, in 1920, the Nichols Company remodeled its property into Spanish-style architecture.

At the same time, the Nichols Company began construction of a series of gasoline filling stations on what were clearly anticipated to be corners in the as-yet-unannounced shopping area. These too received distinctive Spanish-style touches in their otherwise utilitarian architecture.

At the west end of the now-evolving planned shopping district, Nichols acquired several acres from a New York real estate speculator who acquired the land during the 1880s land boom. George Tourtellot had to travel by train to Gotham to complete the transaction. As soon as the title cleared, Nichols leased space to a riding academy. The company built a Spanish-style stable for the academy in Brush Creek valley roughly where the Parkway 600 restaurant is located currently. Many residents in Nichols' subdivisions wished to have their children learn to ride or to board horses for themselves.

WORLD-FAMOUS **COUNTRY CLUB PLAZA**, KANSAS CITY, MO.

Plaza Neighbors: Country Day and Sunset Hill Schools

Concern for education for the children of his home buyers held at least as strong a place for J.C. Nichols as for the shopping needs of their mothers. He worked to upgrade existing schools such as Border Star and Prairie. He also cooperated with mothers who wished to establish private schools for their children.

Vassie James Ward received a college education at Vasser College. Mrs. Ward sought to establish a progressive boys school for her growing sons and those of her neighbors. She patterned it after the country-day school model gaining popularity in the East. The name implied that the location was semi-rural and that the students lived at home rather than boarding in the school.

First classes for Kansas City Country Day School commenced in the fall of 1910. J.C. Nichols donated the use of the old Wornall family residence which he had recently bought for future housing sites. Shortly afterward, Vassie Ward donated land on the north side of Ward Parkway next to State Line Road for a permanent campus for the school. It occupied the present grounds by 1920.

Meanwhile, Mrs. Ward also had a daughter she wished to have educated in a similar private school environment. Together with other ladies in the Nichols neighborhoods, she worked to establish Sunset Hill School, named after the housing subdivision in which she lived and on which the school grounds resided. Once again, Vassie Ward donated the site.

In the case of Country Day School, it was located almost a mile southwest of the Plaza at State Line Road on Ward Parkway. Sunset Hill School constructed its facilities on the hill overlooking the future Plaza location at Wornall Road. Some years later Country Day combined with another boys' school—Pembroke—to form Pembroke Country Day School. Finally, Pembroke Country Day and Sunset Hill combined to form the co-educational private school, Pembroke Hill. Both campuses continue in use. The lower school occupies the Wornall Road campus while the secondary classes occur at the State Line Road location.

Both institutions are older than the Country Club Plaza. Dozens of proms and dances have taken place in and around the Plaza over the last 75 years. The Plaza and Pembroke Hill do indeed make good neighbors for each other!

Profile: Jesse Clyde Nichols

Born in Johnson County, Kan., educated at the University of Kansas (with a scholarship year at Harvard); and toughened by an early failure in land speculation in the Southwest, J.C. Nichols began work in Kansas City, Kan., with determination but little vision. All he and his lawyer partners were doing was providing minimal housing for people fleeing the Kansas River flood-plain homes in which they had been trapped in the 1903 flood.

It is impossible to trace exactly the way in which J.C. Nichols' vision of planned neighborhoods and planned shopping centers evolved. We do know that Park and Boulevard system designer George Kessler had some indirect influence. The two worked for Hugh Ward designing the Sunset Hill subdivision and Ward Parkway beginning in 1907.

Nichols' residential community vision appeared in full form in the *Kansas City Star* in April 1908 when his "1,000 Acres Restricted" were announced. The thousand acres included what ultimately became Mission Hills, Kan., as well as the section adjacent to Kansas City, Mo., stretching from Brush Creek south to 59th and from Brookside to State Line Road. The Missouri properties were annexed into Kansas City, Mo., by court decision in 1911.

Nichols married his high-school sweet-heart, Jessie Miller, in 1905 after both completed college—she at Vassar, just like Vassie James Ward. They set up housekeeping in one of the first houses Nichols constructed in his Missouri development. It had no running water or sewer connection. Water came from a spring a few hundred yards away.

As the three Nichols children—Eleanor, Miller, and Clyde, Jr.—came along, the family moved to three successive locations in the Country Club District. The last move came in 1920 when Nichols repurchased a house the company had built for coal and timber dealer Charles Keith. After moving to 1214 West 55th Street (then called "Santa Fe Road") location, Mr. and Mrs. Nichols never moved again. He died there in 1950. Mrs. Nichols survived him by only a year.

Between 1905 and 1950, J.C. Nichols acquired a national reputation as a builder and developer. He gathered around him young men and women whom he trusted and inspired. The Country Club Plaza has had only 5 property managers over its first 75 years. It is a rare thing when a man starts a company that survives more than 90 years. It is even rarer that the founder was willing to train and delegate enough authority to keep employees for such a period. J.C. Nichols was both visionary and an inspiring boss. The Country Club Plaza continues to hold its position in the hearts and minds of Kansas Citians largely because of those qualities.

J.C. Nichols with Jack Henry. 1934.

One of the true success stories of Plaza stores, Jack Henry opened his first shop in 1931. At the time of this photo with Mr. Nichols he served as president of the Plaza Merchants Association. Henry sold out his interest in the business, but the store still occupied the 1947 site into which it moved upon the opening of the Plaza Time Building in the 1990s

White Eagle Gasoline Station and the Park Lane Apartments [under construction] 1925

From the beginning of the Plaza, plans called for steady revenue-producing stores and for expanding the density of residential population in the immediate neighborhood. Until after World War II, gasoline stations served as the most reliable income sources of all. In particular, rent from service station sites helped the Nichols Company weather the hard times of the Great Depression. Contractors built the Park Lane apartments as one of the first high-rise units within walking distance of the Plaza in the middle 1920s.

Chapter 2:
The Plaza is Announced

READERS OF THE *Kansas City Times* got a look into the future as they perused their morning papers on April 30, 1922. A news story accompanied by a line drawing announced J.C. Nichols' intentions. He was going to build a whole new place to shop and visit at the south end of town.

By that time it was an ill-kept secret. People knew that Nichols had George Tourtellot assembling parcels of land in the neighborhood. They had witnessed the makeover of Chandler's Floral in 1920. That same year a Spanish-styled stable opened as a riding academy on the west end of the land Tourtellot purchased. The hints were all in place.

Still, the scope of the project must have surprised most readers. What they saw in the drawing portrayed seven blocks of store buildings to be constructed in one unified style by one landlord—the J.C. Nichols Company.

Recently arrived architect Edward Buehler Delk did the rendering. In it, he pictured the few existing buildings (Chandler's and several gasoline filling stations) surrounded by much more massive structures. Tall, almost medieval towers stood out at several points. Tile roofs and enclosed inner courtyards or patios frequently appeared. The overview provided a vista unlike anything ever seen in Kansas City or any other U.S. urban center up to that time.

The planning behind the drawing was interesting and complex. Nichols had been consulting with George Kessler since their days of working for Hugh and Vassie Ward on Sunset Hill. Additionally, in 1913, Nichols hired a local man Herbert Hare, as consulting landscape architect. Press releases announced the earliest documented Hare involvement in Plaza planning just prior to the overall announcement at the end of April 1922. For years Nichols had tried to shut down or buy the Lyle Brick Company and Quarry located west of Main Street in the hills overlooking Brush Creek. Finally, early in 1922, through a combination of pressures from courts and George Tourtellot's offers, the 30-year-old concern decided to give in. Nichols announced that Herbert Hare and his father would immediately "commence a study landscaping it for family hotels and high-class apartment buildings."

This press notice indicated what the general Plaza announcement and drawing only hinted at—there was to be more to the Plaza than stores and restaurants. Nichols had Tourtellot buy land in all directions from the initial location on Mill Creek Parkway at 47th Street.

Christmas on the Plaza. 1930.

There is no time like Christmas on the Plaza. Beginning in 1925, Plaza employees strung Christmas lights along the outlines of some buildings. The broader decorating themes of candles, wreaths, visits from Santa in his own house, took hold after 1929.

In the 1990s, upwards of 250,000 line themselves into the streets, walkways, and hotel and apartment locations in and around the Plaza to view the lighting of the Plaza lights. The special event occurs each Thanksgiving night with the nightly display continuing through January 15 of the following year.

Nichols envisioned rows of apartment structures from three-story "walk-ups" to the new style of 9- and 10-story high-rise "apartment hotels" then coming on line in other parts of the city and the nation. The developer had no intention of trying to build apartments as well as stores and "parking stations," as the lots for automobiles were styled in company advertising. Rather, he planned to sell off this adjacent land to construction companies who could assume the financial burden for that essential part of the Plaza mix.

The other members of the planning team included architect Delk and unnamed employees of the Nichols Company. Included in this last group, Edward Tanner probably influenced the growth of the Plaza more than any other member of the organization. Tanner, a young graduate of the University of Kansas, ultimately designed the bulk of the buildings along with Nichol's future son-in-law, Earl Allen.

The press announcement read by Kansas Citians on that April morning painted no small vision. It made it clear that the company was going to do everything both to build up and to serve the immediately surrounding population in the Country Club District. Moreover, it stated the additional goal of attracting customers from "the entire southwestern residential section of Greater Kansas City."

The release concluded by stating what Mr. Nichols and his company considered to be the distinguishing aspect of the plan: "The outstanding

Easter Bunnies, Crestwood Shops. 1922

Without question, the longest-used seasonal decorations on the Plaza are the Easter bunnies—male and female—who stand life-sized on sidewalks and street corners. They first appeared at the Crestwood Shops [55th and Oak] in 1922 and became fixtures at the Plaza in 1931.

Halloween Decorations. 1933.

Christmas and Easter were not the only holidays celebrated on the Plaza in the 1930s. Halloween brought fantastic owls, black cats, witches and pumpkins out of the Nichols Company warehouses.

Aerial View of the Plaza. 1926.

Looking to the north with E.C. White School in the center foreground, this illustration demonstrates progress on the Plaza through the summer of 1926. The first block of buildings [Suydam, Tower, Wolferman's and Barker's Garage lie directly north of Chandler's Nursery and Floral. The Triangle Buildings and Balcony Buildings also stand completed along and north of 47th St. St. Luke's Hospital stands north along Mill Creek [J.C. Nichols] Parkway. The newly completed Liberty Memorial is visible in the upper right hand corner.

Grouping of Plaza Buildings. 1924.

Long the signature buildings of the Plaza, the Suydam [Mill Creek], the Tower, and the Wolferman [Commerce Bank] Buildings framed the north side of the eastern entrance to the Plaza along 47th Street. In the background stands the Barker Brothers Garage [parking structure] while the Sinclair filling station [Fountain Cafe] stands front and center. These buildings have housed a multitude of tenants over the decades. The Suydam, Tower, and Wolferman Buildings, studied independently of their setting, are each an architectural masterpiece in its own right.

feature of these plans is that the ultimately immense project is planned in advance, assuring complete architectural harmony of the buildings, all placed according to landscape and ground plan adopted in advance for the entire area."

Americans have since become so used to the idea of large area project planning that it can be difficult to see why this was so revolutionary at the time. But in 1922, there was almost nothing like this being done anywhere in the country. Only a few planned residential subdivisions approached the scope of Nichols' Country Club District development. Some of these, notably Roland Park in Baltimore, included space for a few shops, as had Nichols. None of them at that time were projecting anything like the 250 shops proposed for the Plaza site.

Nichols' concern for the construction of apartment houses surrounding the proposed development indicates his careful study of what it would

take to make such a grandiose concept work financially. A 1924 company press notice expressed it this way:

"Country Club Plaza, being built at the gateway of the Country Club District, was conceived primarily to serve this rapidly growing community of homes, soon to have a population of 50,000 people. At the same time it is the center of a large amount of vacant land, zoned for apartments and family hotels, which should in a comparatively short time, surround the Country Club Plaza with a more intensive population than exists around any other shopping center in Kansas City."

This last comment is especially telling. It recognizes the existence of other shopping centers in the city at that time. Hence, in their own literature, the Nichols Company did not falsely lay claim to the idea that it was the first shopping center in Kansas City. What the writer knew and wished to convey was that these other centers all depended on connec-

J.C. Nichols Investment Company Steam Shovel at Work. 1926.

The construction of the Knabe Building [housing A/X Armani and the Nature Company in the 1990s] indicated the degree to which the Nichols Company did its own dirt and construction work on the Plaza buildings during its first 70 years. In the background, the Plaza Riding Academy provided both accommodations for Country Club District residents to board their own horses and for District children to learn to ride on the Academy's own mounts. Continued development of the land in Mission Hills and the Brush Creek watershed in the 1930s ended the opportunities for horseback riding in what has become Kansas City's second Downtown.

tions with the streetcar system. A later release put it simply: "The Country Club Plaza has the distinction of being the first major suburban shopping center to be developed away from a transfer or terminal point."

Also, none of the other centers, such as at 31st & Troost or 39th & Main received the type of planning or architectural control provided by one single owner developer. While adjacent stores might feed off the traffic generated by each other in these other shopping areas, the stores had no common thread or planning capability. Their neighbors could either help or cannibalize them. Such was not to be the case in the Plaza.

As land came under his control, in the immediate area planned for the Plaza, he leased sites and built "artistically designed filling stations" for the major oil companies of the day. We do not see most of the names today—SOCONY, Standard, White Eagle, Skelly, and Winters. A few brand names of the stations persist today in altered form: SOCONY is now Mobil; Standard is now Amoco. Still others continue as competitors under the names used in the '20s: Phillips and Sinclair, for example.

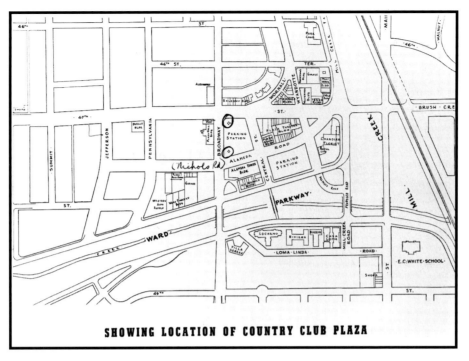

SHOWING LOCATION OF COUNTRY CLUB PLAZA

Map of Building Locations. 1930.

By 1930, Plaza development expanded across 47th Street to include the Plaza Theater block, the J.C. Nichols Building, the Plaza Hall [Knabe] Building, and the Ward Parkway Garage. Additionally, all five high-rise apartment buildings—Casa Loma, Biarritz, Riviera, Locarno, and Villa Serena [Raphael Hotel]—stood completed.

Special attention needs to be paid to the role of the humble gasoline stations in the history of the Plaza and of the Nichols Company as a whole. J.C. Nichols seems to have sensed something of the future impact of the automobile very early in his career. In addition to buying up land connected to the plots he already owned for house building in Kansas City and Johnson County, he went out into the countryside and bought up land at crossroads points across northeastern Kansas and west central Missouri. He gambled on the possible location of major highway routes connecting rural farmland with the growing city.

Other than the Chandler Floral structures and the Riding Academy, these gasoline stations were the first occupants of Plaza land. During the Great Depression of the 1930s, these stations alone generated solid revenues in some years when almost every other business was scarcely surviving. It is just possible that the gasoline stations may have been what kept the entire enterprise afloat in those lean years.

Profile: George Tourtellot

Possibly no other man besides J.C. Nichols himself had as much to do with giving birth and life to the Plaza than this quiet man of French descent. In turn, Tourtellot actively worked for the Nichols Company from 1909 to 1958.

From the middle teens when Nichols developed initial ideas for the Plaza, George Tourtellot was the employee who did what Nichols wanted or couldn't do himself. For example, had J.C. Nichols personally gone to landowners in the future Plaza area and asked to buy their land, prices for vacant lots in the district would have jumped immediately. George Tourtellot quietly approached the same people without raising suspicion concerning the ultimate use of the property and enabled the company to acquire the site piecemeal over a number of years at a reasonable cost.

Near the time of his retirement, Tourtellot recalled a couple of humorous instances during this land-acquisition period. The first involved a family in which he was negotiating with the wife because the husband was opposed to the sale.

As it happened, he was visiting with the wife in their house one afternoon when the husband walked up unexpectedly. The woman told Tourtellot he must leave immediately. The front door was useless—the husband was rapidly approaching the steps. Tourtellot ran out the backdoor only to find a 7-foot fence surrounding the entire backyard with no gate in sight. To the day he counted the story, he wasn't sure how he scaled the fence without attracting the husband's attention, but he made it. A few days later, he and the wife got the husband's signature on a bill of sale.

In a second, even more complicated instance, another husband accused Tourtellot of causing his wife's death. The circumstance came about when Tourtellot purchased a house and lot on the future Plaza site. Part of the agreement was that the owners had permission to move the house since the Company only wanted the land it occupied. The husband and wife then decided to sell the two-story house in two parts. They had the structure sawed in half with the upper story going to one location for remodeling and the main floor destined for a different site entirely.

Problems developed when fall rains slowed progress after the first story was removed. The structure was in a draw leading to Brush Creek. It didn't dry out until the ground froze for the winter, and the opportunity to move the main floor passed until warmer weather. The wife worried so much about the fate of the lower story stuck in the mud that, according to her husband, she died of the aggravation. He promptly visited Tourtellot accusing him of hastening her demise because he bought the house. Of course, Tourtellot pointed out that he had nothing to do with their decision to cut the house in half and move it to different locations, which is what really caused all the delays and presumed frustration for the wife. "Never a dull moment," was his concluding comment to a reporter asking about the incident much later. No suits resulted, but the husband never quite got over it either.

Managing the Plaza leases was a major responsibility. George Tourtellot accomplished the difficult task with grace and equanimity. In many ways, he was the "captain" of the Plaza with J.C. Nichols assuming the more controlling role as "general."

Knabe Building [Armani & The Nature Company]. 1928.

The Nichols Company erected this set of shops across 47th Street from the Wilkie Building [Pottery Barn/Canyon Cafe]. It faced east toward a surface parking. The second floor of this building served as the "Plaza Hall" meeting place during the 1930s. That space was subdivided in doctor, dentist, and professional office space in the 1940s. Edward Tanner was the Knabe Building architect. The Knabe Music Studio occupied the largest space in the structure when it opened—hence the original name.

Profile: Edward Buehler Delk

Born and educated in the East, with a diploma from the University of Pennsylvania, Edward Buehler Delk came to Kansas City at the request of J.C. Nichols just after the Armistice concluding World War I. Nichols chaired a committee for the National Association of Real Estate Boards during the War years. This brought him in contact with a number of the prominent land developers of the East Coast. When Nichols requested a reference for an architect, Delk's name came up.

Delk never served as an employee of the Nichols Company. He always operated as an independent architect who was quite willing to accept commissions to work for J.C. Nichols who brought him to Kansas City in the first place.

In addition to his initial plan for the entire Plaza development, Delk designed the first building erected after the Plaza plan gained public awareness. Constructed facing Mill Creek Boulevard, the Suydam building set the standard for what was to follow.

Delk's design for the Suydam Building received the following description in company notices:

> "'The design of the building at 4638 Mill Creek Parkway portrays the influence of ancient Spain; with roof of tiles in tones of apricot and Indian red; arches with designs of mosaic tile set in buff-colored stucco; a broad horizontal band at the second floor level ornamented by glazed terra cotta in tones of blue, green and yellow; an overhanging roof, gay with brilliant colors...' all made it a most unusual structure for Kansas City."

As the years progressed, Delk continued a close relationship with the company. He did not, however, continue to play a major designing role for the Plaza. That responsibility devolved to young Edward Tanner, Nichols' in-house architect.

Kansas City Gas Company Building [The Nature Company]. 1930.

J.C. Nichols planned the construction of the Giralda Tower attached to this structure in 1929. The onset of the Great Depression led the company to delete the decorative tower from the final design which formed an extension of the Knabe Building [A/X Armani/The Nature Company].

Ward Parkway Garage [Rich Ellison's Plaza Auto Service]. 1928.

Designed both to service cars for Plaza visitors and to store cars for nearby apartment residents, this building has enjoyed continuous use for its original purpose for almost 70 years. It has even appeared in a movie. The 1990 release of Mr. & Mrs. Bridge included a scene in which Mrs. Bridge encountered their son Doug on a date as she waited for her Lincoln to be returned from being serviced. The second level parking area for this garage extended further west in the 1950s with the construction of Milleman's [Plaza III] restaurant.

The Plaza, First and Always

Chapter 3:
Good Things to Eat, See and Do

THERE REALLY IS SOME wiggle room when it comes to deciding what was the first Plaza building. The perennial favorite is the Mill Creek (originally Suydam) Building at 4638 Mill Creek Parkway. A good case can also be made for the Chandler Buildings (1st and 2nd). The first Chandler building on the site had little distinctiveness to it except for its early date (1916). The second, as remodeled, clearly took on more of a Spanish touch but hardly heralded the groundbreaking change in design demonstrated by the Mill Creek structure. The Chandler building was torn down in 1961. The Giralda Tower, The Cheesecake Factory, Mario Triccio and Mark Shale's store now occupy the site.

The other candidates for first building include the several gasoline filling stations erected prior to the announcement in 1922. For gas stations, they are quite distinctive. As enduring pieces of architecture, which heavily influenced subsequent efforts, they fall short just as does the Chandler Building.

One really has to come back to the Mill Creek Building. Edward Beuhler Delk added touches of decoration that allowed for myriad variations in later construction and design. While it is overshadowed by a number of neighbors in the late 1990s, the detail in this building deserves close study even at present.

Almost no one in Kansas City recognizes it as the first structure unless they have done their homework. The primary reason for that fact is that it has been melded into the surrounding structures in such a way as to complete an almost seamless design. What most observers do not realize is that the apparently relatively plain building in the middle facing what is now J.C. Nichols Parkway is really what set the design pattern in motion in the first place. (Mill Creek Parkway was renamed in the developer's honor after his death in 1950.)

The issue of the overall design theme for the Plaza has drawn much speculation. Because Nichols went on a trip to Europe in 1922, many conclude that the trip was the inspiration for the style. Company press releases at the time indicate otherwise. The company spokeswoman, Besse Kibbe Palmer, who doubled as Nichols' secretary at the time, made it clear that he was going to Spain to study architecture because that style had been chosen for the Plaza. In other words, Nichols tailored his vacation plans to meet the needs of the design decision already made, not the other way around.

McCandless Apartments Under Construction. 1928.

Carrying out his original plan of selling land surrounding the intended shopping area for apartment buildings, J.C. Nichols sold all the lots between Mill Creek [J.C. Nichols] Parkway and Wornall Road on the south side of Brush Creek to McCandless Construction Company. This organization, in turn, built the Casa Loma, Biarritz, Riviera, Locarno, and the Villa Serena [Raphael Hotel] units. At the time of this photo, from left to right, only the east side of the Casa Loma, the Locarno and the Villa Serena stood completed.

Mr. and Mrs. Nichols had been planning to visit Europe (without any specified side-trips to the Iberian Peninsula) in 1914. They even got aboard a German-operated ocean liner bound for England. Two days out they felt the ship turn around. They discovered that Germany had declared war on France and was preparing for the same with England. World War I ended the hope of their visit at that time.

So, if Nichols had never seen Spanish architecture in place, where did he come up with the idea? The chances are great that Edward Buehler Delk influenced the decision more than Nichols himself. Delk was definitely the most classically educated person close to Nichols at the time. He did the designs for most of the earliest buildings on the Plaza.

Nichols himself believed strongly in the idea of making each shopping center he owned distinctive in its architectural style. The choice of Spanish-Mediterranean for

Plaza Bank of Commerce [Barami Store]. 1930.

This new bank opened for business under the dome at Alameda [Nichols Rd.] & Central on January 30, 1930. This was not an auspicious time for a new bank, but the directorship overlapped with that of Commerce Trust and included both Mr. Nichols and Mr. Taylor. President Dwight D. Eisenhower's oldest brother, Arthur, served as Plaza Bank president in the early 1950s while continuing as Commerce Trust vice-president.

Plaza Bank of Commerce later moved to the "terrace level" of the Helzberg Building two blocks west on Alameda [Nichols Rd.]. In the 1970s it moved to the current location at 47th & Wyandotte where it operated as a Commerce Bank branch in the 1990s. The Commerce Trust and Commerce Banks have always been led by members of the James Kemper families.

the Plaza may well have been because of the elasticity of the design. In other words, the overall appearance of each building could vary greatly and still be considered part of the coordinated design of the whole center. Regardless of the source of the idea, it has worked wonderfully well for more than 75 years.

Just as interesting as its design, the Mill Creek Building had a delightful parade of early occupants. Indeed, the first four tenants to sign a lease were business-women. Nichols wanted to appeal to the women in his residential sections. How better to do this than to attract businesses run by women and offering goods and services for women?

The pioneer in the project was Miss Reineke's Photography Studio. As a portrait photographer, this woman of German extraction began her business in down-town Kansas City. A Nichols company press release noted, "Miss Reineke feels that she is placing herself in a better position to care for her patrons, who include, besides children, many of the leading business men of Kansas City." Part of Nichols' strategy already took hold. At least one downtown merchant recognized the value of operating closer to where her customers lived.

Following Miss Reineke's lease, Mrs. M.C. Chisholm's Millinery Shop, Mrs. J.C. McGavran's Marinello Beauty Shop, and the Lu-Frances Baby Shop took space as well. Suydam Furniture and Interior Decorating moved into the largest shop space in the building in August 1923. Both Miss Reineke and Mrs. McGavran continued operating businesses on the Plaza for decades into the future.

Even before the leases were signed on the Mill Creek Building in 1923, the Nichols Company commenced construction on the Triangle Building, located almost a block away and surrounded by 47th Street, Wyandotte, and Wornall Road. Unlike the two-story Mill Creek Building, the Triangle shops were always intended as single-story locations. Early tenants in the Triangle block included the "Sign of the Thistle Shop," dedicated to gifts and accessories; Jane Nichols (no relation) Lingerie; Superior Cleaners and Western Union Telegraph.

At almost the same time that construction commenced on the Triangle block, Nichols Company workers began excavation for the Wolferman Building. The slogan of Fred Wolferman was always "Good Things to Eat." He and J.C. Nichols intended his Plaza store to be his masterpiece. Wolferman began grocery operations downtown near the turn of the century. By 1923 he had a number of stores scattered throughout the city. They were primarily grocery and produce markets although some also contained a meat market, still unusual for a grocery store in the '20s.

The Plaza Wolferman's had all that, and more. The most noticeable addition, besides abundant space, appeared in the form of an in-store bakery or "cookery" department, as described in press releases at the time. Schulze Baking Company operated the new department under contract with Wolferman. This store had all the elements of the modern supermarket—something historians usually ascribe to the 1930s for its origin.

Everything was up to date at Fred Wolferman's...and on the Plaza!

According to the J.C. Nichols Company, Fred Wolferman was initially less than enthusiastic about putting a store "out South." J.C. Nichols used his considerable powers of persuasion to no avail for some time. Then he learned that Mr. and Mrs. Wolferman planned a trip by rail to the West Coast. Nichols purchased a round-trip ticket on the same train. He literally sold the Plaza location to the Wolfermans all the way out and all the way back. Upon return, the deal was struck. There would be a Wolferman's at the Plaza, but in Wolferman's own building. Later, when Wolferman's closed, James Kemper, Jr. of Commerce Bank bought the structure to turn it into the Plaza Bank of Commerce's main location. Mr. Wolferman's insistence turned the building into one of two major structures on the Plaza not currently owned and leased by the Nichols Company in the late 1990s. (The other is the Skelly building).

Early in 1924, Nichols Company public relations notices indicated that "several streets in the Plaza (will be provided) with wider paving than is to be found on any street in Kansas City." The primary purpose of the additional space at that time was to allow automobiles to angle park against the curb. Given the overall lower volume of traffic, it was not necessary to allow for two lanes of traffic going each direction. The width of streets described is exactly the same as the street widths in the 1990s. The difference is that much more street parking took place because almost two cars can angle park in the curb length than one car can parallel park.

The press release also noted that approximately 50% of the total land area of the Plaza would be devoted to streets, loading areas and parking spaces. This was quite a different allocation of space compared to Downtown Kansas City or at any of the shopping centers sprung up along streetcar line transfer corners. In the previous shopping areas, the premium was on having enough showroom space. Previous merchants (and their landlords) expected shoppers to arrive and depart by streetcar so little consideration need be given for auto parking. Downtown merchants maintained this parking-avoidance position well into the 1950s.

Nichols actually advocated creating more than enough parking places for the Plaza in the early years. Partly, he could afford to do so—he had more land than tenants. Partly, he believed that by doing so, he could encourage automobile traffic which meant that Plaza customers would be among the more affluent Kansas Citians of the time. Then, after World War II as the whole urban area seemed to wish to satisfy its car hunger all at once, Nichols was right where he wanted to be—controlling shops which had plenty of curbside or nearby parking to every store in the Plaza. Downtown merchants woke up too late, started tearing down more buildings than necessary with Urban Renewal dollars, and actually created too much parking by the early '70s. By then, Nichols and mall developers had won the war.

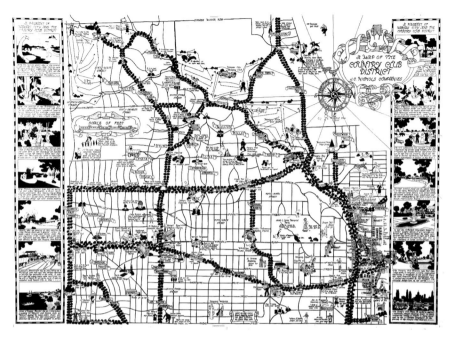

Cartoon Map of the Country Club District. 1930.

Drawn to decorate the west wall of the lobby of the new J.C. Nichols store-front at 310 Ward Parkway, this map illustrates the extent of Nichols Company developments as of September, 1930. Company architect, Earl Allen drew the map in close detail. Visitors can view the large diagram in the Nichols Company offices any time during regular business hours. One 1995 critical reviewer suggested that the information contained on the map indicated the official J.C. Nichols Company interpretation of Kansas City history in their neighborhoods.

Shortly after this time, Allen married J.C. Nichols' oldest child, Eleanor. A fountain on Nichols Road facing Eddie Bauer's is dedicated to their memory.

attention to parking needs then, just as he was doing. Possibly understandably, but certainly in a shortsighted way, those merchants chose to give their competitor a deaf ear. After all wasn't this the guy who was wooing away some of their own in little bits and pieces? Who does what their enemy advises? Certainly not the big department stores and Downtown chain-store managers.

As large apartment houses arose next to or near the Plaza, Nichols sought to accommodate the automobile storage needs of these residents by constructing large garages where the vehicles could be stored and serviced all at once. The first of these opened in 1923 in an Edward Buehler Delk-designed structure behind the Mill Creek building. Operated by Barker Brothers who ran other such facilities elsewhere in the city, this building was capable of storing over 100 cars at a time.

There is an irony in all this. As early as the 1920s, Nichols offered unsolicited advice to Downtown merchants. He told them they needed to pay

At the Plaza, the garages continued to be greatly used through the 1920s, but toward the end of the decade somewhat fewer people wanted to rent garage space when they could park their cars outside on the street for free. The Barker Garage did not survive the Great Depression in its original use.

One other garage location proved more enduring. The Ward Parkway garage opened in 1928 with space to park or store up to 275 vehicles. Though altered in some ways, the garage still operates in the late 1990s at 420 Ward Parkway.

As the buildings on the Plaza continued to accumulate—the Tower building, the Balcony building, the Knabe building, Ward Parkway Garage and the Plaza Theater—Nichols realized that angle parking along the streets was not sufficient. Two "parking stations" opened on the south side near Brush Creek. The first of these stood where Hall's is now located. The second actually continues in use, although altered in form, in the block between Central and Broadway, 47th to Nichols Road. Initially, they were simply walled-in parking areas.

One of J.C. Nichols' great hopes at the outset was for the Plaza to serve as a shopping center for the entire surrounding region as well as for the residents in the more immediate area. To this end, he lobbied state and national lawmakers to designate Ward Parkway to the west and Brush Creek Parkway to the east as a Federal Highway in the late 1920s. Ultimately, he succeeded. U.S. Highway 50 arrived from central Missouri by way of Blue and Brush Creek Parkways. It exited the city to the west following Ward Parkway and present-day Shawnee Mission Parkway as far as Metcalf Road where it abruptly turned south and later southwest. In the 1990s, this route was known as U.S. Highway 56, which more or less paralleled the Santa Fe Trail from Prospect Ave. (U.S. 71) in Kansas City to Santa Fe, NM. For Nichols, the highway connection meant increased traffic for the Plaza and its merchants. He reasoned that if vehicles traveled by the stores, the drivers might very well stop in to make a purchase.

Holidays in american life have tended to spark additional buying of gifts and clothing. Early on, Nichols recognized the importance of Christmas in stimulating sales. Within two years of the opening of the first stores (or by 1925), Christmas trees and thousands of colored lights began to be placed around the buildings. This tradition has grown to the point in the 1990s where the lighting of the Plaza Lights on Thanksgiving night is one of the most densely attended events in the entire metropolitan area. In the 1990s upwards of 250,000 gather in the streets and sidewalks to see the instant when 250,000 lights on over 75 miles of wiring spark to life.

By the 1930s, visits to Santa Claus came along. Maintenance personnel erected a special Santa house on the then-vacant lot behind the Ward Parkway Garage facing Alameda (Nichols Road). Youngsters and their parents could visit the house to share Christmas wishes with St. Nick.

Easter also came to be an important holiday. The purchase of new clothes for spring and of flower and garden merchandise served to open the long warm-weather season in late March or early April. As early as 1931, the Nichols maintenance people placed human-sized painted bunnies at the corners in the Crestwood Shopping Center at 55th & Oak. In 1931 these bunnies and their oversized Easter eggs became fixtures on the Plaza. The custom is still being observed in the late 1990s.

Halloween and Thanksgiving came in for their share of Plaza decorations in the '20s and '30s as well. Oversized witches and pumpkins supplied part of the atmosphere in the small park in front of the Plaza Theater or on vacant lots toward the west end of the Plaza. Through the summer a pony ring operated for decades with Shetland Pony rides furnished by R.L. Fish in the late 1920s. Fish was reputed to own the largest group of Shetland ponies in the United States at that time.

From the time of the initial announcement of the Plaza, J.C. Nichols contemplated the construction of a grand movie theater to challenge the beauty of any of the Downtown theaters such as the Midland, the Empire, and the Uptown. In March 1928, excavation got underway for the construction of the Plaza Theater. Designed by Nichols' own architect, Edward Tanner, in consultation with Boller Brothers, architects, the Plaza Theater opened October 9, 1928, with great fanfare. Shops went in on both sides but facing outwards to provide a strong economic underpinning to the Theater operation. The Fox chain provided the initial management contractors.

Profile: Edward Tanner

A product of the University of Kansas, like Nichols himself, Ed Tanner joined the Company after World War I. He participated in the initial planning for the Plaza in a variety of ways, including designing the remodeling of Chandler's Floral and Nursery in 1920. Twice in the 1920s, his designs won awards from the Architectural League of Kansas City—in 1927 for the Knabe Building (housing A/X Armani and the Nature Company in the 1990s), and in 1929 for the Plaza Theater.

Over the decades, Tanner mastered the design style for the Plaza. He learned how to specify details that made brand-new buildings appear instantly as though they had stood for decades or even centuries. His sense of the proportions necessary to keep the Plaza on a human scale was absolutely necessary as the company sought to expand "bigger and better." Fortunately for Nichols, he also knew how to design and build within a budget of time and money. Between Tanner and fellow company architect, Earl Allen, most of the facades of Plaza buildings constructed between 1922 and 1950 bore a remarkable conformity to the overall design while maintaining necessary individuality.

Tanner moved up to a position as vice-president of the company in later years. At certain points, such as in the Depression and World War II, he set up an architectural shop technically independent of the Nichols Company in order to compete for needed government design contracts or to stop the drain on company payroll resources.

Regardless, Tanner's capabilities found their greatest expression in Plaza structures. George Tourtellot was the "Captain" of the Plaza through his designs. J.C. Nichols served as "General" of the Plaza through his controlling vision. Edward Tanner deserves at least the title of "Lieutenant" for all the yeoman-like work he did to create a unified Plaza look and feel over the years.

Plaza Christmas Lights. 1932.

As the Great Depression deepened, it seemed that more lights proved necessary to dispell the gloom. In this worst of all Depression years when Christmas fell between the defeat of Herbert Hoover and the inauguration of Franklin Delano Roosevelt, the Plaza lights shown across 47th Street in garlands as well as along the outlines of Plaza buildings.

The only time in which the Plaza lights were curtailed occurred in 1973 when President Nixon called upon all Americans to curtail the use of Christmas lights to reduce American dependence on foreign oil imports.

Chapter 4: The Plaza Weathers the Great Depression

THE FIRST FULL YEAR OF the Great Depression signified the submission of the Plaza to one of the crazes of the era—miniature golf. As economic times worsened, people wanted less expensive entertainment. While wealthy families continued to enjoy the real thing, many Plaza goers made do with golf's wonderful imitation. "Tom Thumb" courses appeared at 47th and Pennsylvania and at 47th & Main Street near the main entrance.

The Depression also took its toll on plans for the Plaza. In 1929, Nichols had his architect son-in-law, Earl Allen design a building he projected for the south side of Broadway with a tall Spanish-style tower anchoring the south end. As the Depression deepened, Nichols went ahead with the building, but left the Tower plans on the drawing room floor. Not until the construction of the Swanson's building in the 1960s did Miller Nichols resurrect that sketch done by his brother-in-law and proceed to construct the Plaza trademark Giralda Tower at 47th and Ward Parkway.

In addition to the new portion of the Knabe building which opened without Allen's tower, the J.C. Nichols Company for the first time moved into its own offices within the Country Club District. In 1905,

Nichols started selling "Country Club District" lots from offices with his partners, the brothers Reed, in the New York Life Building downtown. When he set up his own company in 1908, they established offices in the Commerce Trust building a few blocks to the east. Thus, 25 years after starting downtown, Nichols brought his own company offices to the Plaza in 1930.

The Nichols Company building was designed to offer shop storefronts on the entire Ward Parkway side in order to earn revenue. Except for one storefront entrance at 310 Ward Parkway, all the Nichols Company offices were on the second floor or in the basement. Later, a third story was added; sometimes employees referred to that third floor as "Mr. Nichols' penthouse." The company still utilizes the same offices in the late 1990s.

While one might expect that all construction on the Plaza would stop during the economic hard times, that was not true. In addition to the J.C. Nichols Company building on Ward Parkway, Meyer's Barbeque Restaurant opened in a separate building in 1931. New buildings went up on the south side of Alameda (Nichols) Road in 1932. Bo Sing's Chinese Restauarant opened in one of these locations in 1932.

Excavation for the Plaza Medical Building (behind the Nichols Company building and facing Alameda) began in November 1936. Also that year, the Circle Building opened to connect the Tower Building on

Parking Stations. 1931.

Plaza stores always had "front door" parking. Originally it was all diagonal parking as it remained on west 48th St. between Pennsylvania and Jefferson. Because of the need for wider street area for four-lane driving, most of the on-street parking was parallel in the 1990s. As early as the late 1920s, fenced-in "parking stations" proved necessary to receive the increased volume of shoppers on busy days.

At one time in the 1950s, Kansas City, Mo., officials sought to place parking meters at each Plaza on-street parking place as a revenue enhancement measure. The Nichols Company and the Plaza Merchants Association fought the idea successfully so that almost all parking space continued to be free to Plaza visitors.

In this particular photo, the wall hides the auto parking spaces while forming a backdrop for the decorative concrete bench in the foreground. Nowhere else in Kansas City [or the United States, at the time] did one find such elaborate parking areas for cars.

47th Street with the Mill Creek Building facing Mill Creek Boulevard. Gerhardt Furs began an occupancy that year which lasted until 1995 when the Circle Building converted to the Fountain Café. That amounted to a Depression-era business succeeding for almost 60 years in the same Plaza location.

The initial phase of the Skelly Building, constructed to house the Tulsa oil company's marketing department, opened in 1938. This proved to be a second Plaza structure not owned and controlled by the company. Nichols consented to its construction because he believed it added prestige and potential customers for Plaza shops during the noon hour and after 5:00 p.m. Also, the money Skelly paid for the land didn't hurt the cash flow either.

The Skelly connection is a reminder of one of the key factors enabling the Nichols Company to survive the Great Depression. All the stores were on a percentage lease. This

Postal Life and Casualty Building. [Talbott's] 1930.

The Nichols Company sought architectural uniformity in the buildings constructed on the Plaza. This insurance company wanted a structure that would represent the solid financial nature of its business. Ultimately, it looked much more like a bank than the building constructed at approximately the same time for the Plaza Bank of Commerce. It did not fit well with the other buildings around it, including its closest neighbor, Chandler Floral.

The building continued in use in the late 1990s with an altered facade as the site of Talbott's. The construction of the parking structure for Swanson's [Mark Shale] in 1967 shielded the back of the building from view. The alterations to the storefront completed to satisfy Talbott's needs converted the former "sore thumb" into a quite harmonious building which "fits" well within its overall surroundings.

meant they paid a pre-negotiated percentage of their gross sales to the Nichols Company in monthly installments. In spite of a brave front, the company actually received much lowered revenues from leases and almost none from housing sales and resales. The bright spot proved to be revenues generated by the several Nichols Company-leased gasoline filling stations scattered about the Plaza, the city and the region.

When most other businesses cut back, the oil companies maintained good cash flow and balance sheets from their petroleum sales. On the Plaza itself, the gasoline stations supplied the greatest volume of business of any Plaza retail outlets.

Even those impressive facts did not fully convince Mr. William T. Kemper at Commerce Bank that the Plaza would survive. In the summer of 1937, when J.C. Nichols and his family were touring South America to allow Nichols recuperation from nervous exhaustion (a

Brush Creek and the Plaza. 1933.

The histories of these two entities, one natural and one entirely man-made, are completely entwined in Kansas City. Brush Creek most of the time is a small tributary of the Blue River. The Plaza developed from 1923 into the oldest suburban automobile-accessed shopping center in America. The scene above pictures a tranquil creek crossed by an old foot bridge.

Shortly after this photo was taken, Brush Creek was transformed from a meandering creek with trees and brush lining its irregular banks into a channelized creek with a concrete bed. Not surprisingly, the concrete for Brush Creek came from the trucks of Tom Pendergast's Red-D-Mixed Concrete Company. The purpose of the pavement was to prevent any future flooding.

recurring problem throughout his life), William T. Kemper called company president, J.C. Taylor, and wanted to examine the company's books. Even though, or maybe because of, the fact that the Nichols Company had a great deal of borrowed money from Commerce Trust, Mr. Taylor steadfastly refused to turn over the company accounting information.

He also placed a long-distance call to J.C. Nichols in Argentina. Nichols told Taylor he was doing the right thing, and to hold off Kemper until he could return to face Kemper personally. That confrontation took place in Kemper's office early in the fall of 1937. Nichols went to see the banker, but did not take his accounting ledgers with him. Instead, when he entered the office, he placed huge rings of keys on Kemper's desk. Nichols is reputed to have said, "There, if you want the Plaza, you can have every last store!"

Kemper rushed around the desk to assure Nichols that the bank had no such desire. Nichols gathered up the key rings and left. Kemper, who died a year later, never saw the "sacred books." Had he done so, he might

**J.C. Nichols and Daughter, Eleanor Nichols Allen.
1936 Plaza Fiesta.**

As Kansas City and the United States fought to overcome the effects of the Great Depression in the mid-1930s, the Plaza hosted a summer celebration known as the Fiesta. It proved such a success that Downtown Kansas City copied the promotion with its "Jubilesta" festivities.

Possibly the most memorable aspect of the gaiety was caught by the company photographer in this remarkable picture. J.C. Nichols usually appeared in public in tailored suits and conducted himself with practiced solemnity. On this occasion, he allowed himself to be photographed with his oldest adult child in a ridiculous sombrero and with his fake mustache slightly askew.

have grabbed the keys. The J.C. Nichols Company was none too healthy financially.

But, as things gradually improved economically in the late '30s and with the onset of World War II, Nichols' most important device for success of the shopping center brought the company back to solvency. That innovation was the percentage lease. While it didn't generate income from some businesses during the Depression (6.5% of nothing is still nothing, in the case of floundering retailers), it enabled the company to benefit from the revenue generated at the gas stations and in a few other instances. As business resumed, the percentage lease enabled the company to benefit right along with their tenants.

Of course, the 1930s were also the heyday of the Pendergast Machine. The full story of the level of cooperation between J.C. Nichols and Kansas City mayor, Tom Pendergast, will never be entirely known. It is clear that the Plaza landlord had nothing to do with the illegal gambling and extortion activities of the machine. It is also clear that from the 'teens through the middle 1930s, Nichols (and

Kroger Store [Brooks Brothers] Opening. November 18, 1946.

Following World War II, Plaza construction increased markedly. This building opened adjoining the Plaza Bowl location to provide the second full-service food supermarket [in addition to Wolferman's] on the Plaza. By the 1960s, Muehlebach Brothers acquired the lease and operated the store until the late 1970s and the coming of Brooks Brothers and Saks. Muehlebach's then moved to the location on Jefferson Street operated in the 1990s as Meiner's Plaza Market.

The Plaza, First and Always

other businessmen, citywide) cooperated with Pendergast in order to get on with daily business. The Nichols Company did, after all, build both Pendergast houses in the Country Club District.

On one front, Pendergast moved a little more rapidly than Nichols probably wanted, although, once again, the result was mutually beneficial—for awhile at least. The issue was Brush Creek and public improvements. In 1930, Kansas City was already losing jobs. It also badly needed updating of public facilities. The proposed solution came in the form of a bond election to approve the city's borrowing enough money to build a new city hall, 2 county courthouses, Municipal Auditorium, a new city market, hundreds of miles of pavement for Jackson County roads, and…a flood control project for Brush Creek.

Brush Creek defined Nichols' early real estate activities profoundly. It was the boundary over which he jumped to start offering houses and lots in 1905. It was the source of the rough land forms in what became Mission Hills after 1908. And, it formed the southern boundary of his retail shops in the Country Club Plaza. Most of the time it was a docile little stream. When spring rains came, and as more of its watershed had streets and houses constructed over it (mostly by the Nichols Company), it could occasionally become a raging torrent. The bond committee considered the danger. Both Nichols and Pendergast served on the Committee of 1,000 drumming up support for the bond election.

Nichols thought he had the Brush Creek plan dropped off the ballot proposition. Right before the election, Henry McElroy, the Pendergast city manager, personally restored the proposal to the total package. The voters approved the proposal and thousands of yards of Pendergast Red-D-Mixed concrete went into the straightened channel. Almost immediately, local wags suggested that more than a few dead bodies may have been interred as well.

The result proved surprisingly satisfactory. The little stream carried its water quickly down a center trough the size of a corn field irrigation ditch. No mosquito breeding pools were left. When it rained heavily in Johnson County, the water moved rapidly and safely past the Plaza. Pendergast profited from the concrete sale, Nichols' Plaza got a generally improved waterway to see and appreciate at flood times. In the 1970s and '80s, the dry summers created the opportunity to use the concrete creek bed for outdoor concerts for much of the city on Sunday afternoons.

By 1937, how well or not the working relationship between Nichols and Pendergast may have operated before, it came to a screeching halt. Nichols experienced labor problems for the first time as the Plaza Medical building proceeded. He apparently complained to City Hall and City Manager McElroy, who also lived in a Nichols-constructed house. McElroy did not supply any assistance. Instead, he announced publicly the possibility of the city building a viaduct for Broadway that would begin at 46th Street and stretch clear across the Plaza and Brush Creek valley to 49th Street and Wornall Road. Had McElroy's outlandish idea actually been accomplished, the Plaza would have been sitting under the supports for this preposterous bridge.

As it happened, Mr. Pendergast and Mr. McElroy had problems of their own brewing with grand juries looking into past elections and into Pendergast's personal fianances. The investigations resulted by 1938 in the purging of tens of thousands of names of dead or fictitious people off the voting rolls. Then, in 1939, Tom Pendergast pled guilty to income tax evasion. He served a year in Leavenworth Federal Penitentiary. The viaduct over the Plaza was forgotten.

Another pioneering aspect of Plaza development came with the organization in 1929 of the Plaza Merchants Association. Patterned after the Homeowners' Associations in Nichols neighborhoods, the Merchants' Association was intended to provide tenants with an avenue for input in the management of the entire shopping area and was created as an entirely seperate corporation.

Promotion of the Plaza is the responsibility of the Merchants' Association. All advertising, marketing, public relations and special events conducted for the Plaza as a whole is coordinated by the

Plaza Art Fair. 1935.

Begun in the depths of the Great Depression, the Plaza Art Fair continued as the shopping district's premier special event in the 1990s. At one time conducted in the springtime, it has long been a feature of the Plaza's September schedule. Plaza merchants always fear rain, and frequently find their fears justified. In 1977, the "Plaza Flood" occurred the week before the schedule art show and sale. In spite of that disaster, it took place in the unflooded portions of the Plaza as scheduled.

Rain or shine, the Plaza Art Fair attracts artists and artisans from across the nation to show their wares to an appreciative buying clientele approaching 100,000 over three days.

Association. These efforts include the placement of the colorful Plaza banners, the Plaza Art Fair and the Plaza holiday lighting ceremony. The association operates from dues paid by all the retail tenants throughout the Plaza.

The Plaza merchants support one another and work cooperatively through the Association while maintaining a competitive atmosphere in their day-to-day operations. The Association does not become involved in lease negotiations of any members. Those are individual arrangements between each merchant and the Nichols Company. The Association does, however, strive to create the type of shopping atmosphere that will encourage sales growth among all member merchants.

Plaza merchants, through their association, encourage each other to publish proper and truthful advertising of merchandise; provide direction and education opportunities for the merchants; and maintain positive relationships with the Convention and Visitors Bureau of Greater Kansas City, the Chamber of Commerce and city government officials.

In the late 1990s, few shopping centers in the United States operate with such an organization because in most cases marketing is provided by the developer through a marketing fund. In the 1920s, the idea was unique. Hence, just as the Plaza itself paved the way for much of modern retailing practice, the Plaza Merchants' Association served as a model for shops areas and malls from that time to the present.

Feature: The Plaza Art Fair

The idea of going to a shopping center on certain occasions to see the handiwork of local artists and crafts people is so commonplace in the 1990s as to be unremarkable. In 1932, however, this was something new and quite different.

It didn't start out as much. There were a few booths with artists displaying their paintings and such. Some years the weather was its usual unpredictable self in Kansas City, but the tradition stuck. The Plaza Art Fair has evolved into one of the premier such events in the Midwest. Artists and crafts workers submit samples or pictures of their work to skilled juries who select what they believe is the finest or most unique examples placed before them. The artists come from many parts of the country to display their wares.

Originally, it ran from a Saturday to the following Thursday. In more recent years, the fairs have settled into a pattern of opening on Friday afternoons and closing by 5:00 p.m. on Sunday. Many living rooms in Kansas City and the surrounding region display pictures, sculpture, or pottery originally spied by the homeowner at the Plaza Art Fair. There have been many imitators (including the Nichols Company's own Brookside Art Fair in the springtime), but there was only one original Plaza Art Fair. The tradition continues!

Nichols Company Leaders Celebrate the Opening of Putsch's 210 [Fedora 210]. March 19, 1947.

Pictured with their wives, [from left] Mrs. Tourtellot, George Tourtellot, Plaza manager; Mrs. Taylor, James S. Jackson, Kansas City Star real estate editor; J.C. Taylor, Nichols Company president; and Ed Tanner, Plaza architect and Nichols Company director; at the opening of one of the all-time favorite Plaza restaurants.

Putsch's 210 became the first of five food and beverage service locations for Jud Putsch. After successfully establishing this operation, they later opened Putsch's Cafeteria, [Houston's Barbeque], Putsch's Coffee House [Sharper Image], the Celler Door, and Putsch's Sidewalk Cafe [Classic Cup]. Amazingly, in the 1960s Putsch operated all five of these businesses within one and one-half blocks of each other without competing with himself.

Plaza Neighbors: The Nelson-Atkins Museum of Art and the University of Kansas City

The year 1933 seems a peculiar time for founding civic institutions. In most parts of the U.S., including Kansas City, residents worked to forget most aspects of the year. Bank holidays, even more wide-spread unemployment, and drought in the wheat and corn country gave few people respite from the trauma of deprivation.

In Kansas City, the bond-issue construction programs already helped alleviate some of the worst unemployment. One of the projects under construction at the same time, but separately funded, the Nelson-Atkins Museum of Art, long known inaccurately as "the Nelson Gallery of Art," opened in 1933. As it happens, J.C. Nichols had a good deal to do with the event. In the late 1920s, conservators of two trusts endowing the new institution appointed him along with two other men as Trustees. Nichols continued to serve in that capacity almost until his death in 1950.

The collections and the architecture of the Museum, jointly endowed by the William Rockhill Nelson family (founders of the Kansas City Star), and Mary McAfee Atkins, continue to inspire and excite visitors to the present. Few remember that the institution was really a product of those difficult times in the 1930s. The addition of outdoor statuary and the construction of a separate Kemper Museum of Contemporary Art nearby have only added to the respect held for the institution by local residents and art critics nationally.

The University of Kansas City, now known as the University of Missouri-Kansas City, was really a gift to the city by William Volker, also one of the original Trustees of the Nelson-Atkins Museum. Mr. Volker, a German immigrant who created a most successful window blind and sash business, gave away money to individuals and worthy causes during his entire life. He bought the land and the first building for the university. He established it as a private institution with a very public purpose.

It became the center for bringing together professional schools such as Law, Dentistry, Pharmacy, and Education, which began separately a decade earlier. That purpose broadened in 1963 when it became part of the public University of Missouri system and a Medical School added to its professional grouping.

Thus, while 1933 may not have been a very good year in many places, it was a beginning for some quite important neighbors to the Plaza. Both are just downstream (or east) along or overlooking Brush Creek within walking distance of the shopping center.

The various cultural institutions, such as UMKC, Linda Hall Library, Midwest Research Institute and the Nelson-Atkins Museum all create an unusual and valuable resource for the metropolitan area and are, in turn, benefited by their proximity to the Country Club Plaza.

Dedication of Aleman Court. May 7, 1947

Plaza Merchants Association president, Barney Barnard, read a dedication statement in the presence of Mexican President Miguel Aleman. Such events help bring validity to the Latin quality of the Plaza ambiance.

Chapter 5
The Heart and Soul of Kansas City

WORLD WAR II ENDED the Great Depression. For the Plaza, however, the War was more stringent than the Depression. The pace of new building construction and new merchant arrivals certainly slowed between 1930 and 1941, but occasional flurries of activity came and went. During the War, new construction proved impossible while merchant changeover seldom occurred.

All that is not to say that 1942-45 was a stagnant period at the Plaza. People had more money to spend even if there was less on which to spend it. Rationing of all sorts drove store managers to creative lengths simply to keep products on the shelves. Prices stayed fairly constant—the result of wartime controls. In many respects, on the home front, the War period was one of biding time.

But, J.C. Nichols was not a man who bided his time at any point in his life. As early as 1940, he went to Washington, D.C., as a "dollar-a-year" man. What that meant is that he worked for a government agency for no salary, save the ceremonial dollar necessary to bind the contract. In Nichols' case he worked for a war-preparedness board which evolved into the War Production Board. The idea was to create enough manufacturing and distribution capacity for the U.S. to be ready to enter the growing European and Asian conflict whenever it spilled into our bailiwick.

Nichols became so adept at getting appointments with strategically important agency and military leaders that others marveled at his access. According to son Clyde, the answer was simple. Nichols took pairs of nylon hose, which were newly on the market, with him when he went personally to make appointments. The nylons went to the receptionist or secretary in charge of making appointments, and Nichols got in almost immediately. Paying attention to the needs of even the front line employee was a lesson Nichols learned well back in Kansas City.

If there was no construction activity going on at the Plaza during World War II, things certainly changed rapidly during post-war demobilization. While the fighting was winding down in Europe and the Pacific, J.C. Nichols and George Tourtellot planned ahead. They were in regular contact with officials of Sears, Roebuck & Company in Chicago. Up to this time, Sears maintained its mail-order business first and foremost. It had catalog shops in many cities and towns. It even had a few larger retail stores close to downtown areas, but it had never gone into the

J.C. Nichols at Work with Secretary Ethel Treshadding. 1948.

Always a high energy person, Nichols conducted a great portion of his business with the elements illustrated. The telephone was essential. Nichols used the instrument to wheedle, cajole, negotiate, and direct his far-flung interests throughout the metropolitan region and on the national stage. Among real estate dealers and land developers, J.C. Nichols was the perceived "Dean" of the profession by the end of World War II.

Given his frequent public speaking engagements, Nichols relied heavily on ideas and editing done by Ms. Treshadding. According to family traditions, Mrs. Jessie Nichols frequently went over his speeches and articles before delivery as well.

The letter being dictated also symbolizes the degree to which Nichols used letters and notes to get his ideas across.

Finally, Ms. Treshadding proved important after the death of Nichols in 1950. She went through his files, summarized what she believed was most important, and destroyed the vast majority of J.C. Nichols' numerous vertical files of correspondence. The reason behind the destruction is not clear, but the loss was catastrophic to those interested in learning more about the life of this unique entrepreneur.

Sears First Christmas Decorations. 1947

The arrival of Sears on the Plaza in 1947 marked a much increased scale of retail activity. For the first time, a full-line department store located somewhere in Kansas City other than Downtown. The Christmas decorations indicate the degree to which the national retailer entered fully into all activities of the Merchants' Association and the Plaza in general.

Mindlin's on the Plaza. 1960.

Mindlin's was a long-time fashion fixture on the Plaza. At this particular time the store operated at 47th and Wyandotte next door to the entrance to the Plaza Theater.

department store business directly in a big way.

Nichols and Gen. Robert Wood, president of Sears, carried on high-level negotiations while George Tourtellot maintained the day-to-day contact with Sears' middle management people. When the War ended, agreement in principle was at hand. Finally, in February 1946, everything fell into place. At the end of the month excavation crews began their work for the Sears contractors.

Downtown business people expressed grave concern over this development. Up to this time in Kansas City, as elsewhere over the country, large department stores operated almost entirely in downtown locations where the public transit lines—both trolley and bus lines—intersected to bring the greatest concentration of shoppers. Sears' plans for the Plaza sent shock waves through that conventional wisdom.

Nichols withstood the criticism and no doubt gloried in the publicity gained with the construction of Sears. On December 1, 1947, *Time Magazine* carried a story about the opening of the Sears location, the Country Club Plaza and Nichols himself. His closing comment in the story demonstrates his philosophy honed by decades of experience in land development and by the Cold War:

"At 67, 'J.C.' Nichols, whose holdings are conservatively estimated at $15,000,000, lives with his wife in a mansion in the Country Club District (his two sons are in the building business), but he still spends most of his days and three evenings a week behind his office desk on city planning projects. J.C. thinks they are of prime importance because

'when you rear children in a good neighborhood, they will go out and fight communism.'"

More than just a massive new Sears store appeared on the Plaza right after V-J day. In rapid succession, the Plaza Time building, the Plaza Bowl, a new Kroger grocery next to the Bowl, all went up in short order. By 1948, additional structures along Alameda (Nichols) Road on both sides west of Broadway came on line.

One of these housed the Plaza Cafeteria in a novel location. The Nichols Company advertised it as a "terrace shop;" it was in fact in a basement location. The public gained access by entering a street level door some 50 feet west of Broadway. They descended stairs to the restaurant level. Unfortunately, as a memo from J.C. Taylor explains, the food in the cafeteria never quite met expectations. In the early 1950s, the Plaza Bank of Commerce (now home of Country Club Bank) took over the location when they moved from the domed structure they had occupied at Central and Alameda since 1930.

Helzberg's "House of Treasures" opened in their current location on the corner of Broadway and Alameda in 1948, immediately adjacent to the Plaza Cafeteria entrance. This store is among the longest lived in one location on the entire Plaza. Immediately across the street, Jack Henry moved to his new location in the Plaza Time building in 1947. This men's wear shop continues in the same location in the late 1990s, albeit under different ownership.

The Pre-Giralda Entrance to the Plaza at Christmastime. 1955

During the decades of Chandler's on the Plaza, this scene greeted Plaza shoppers from the 1920s through the 1950s. The Plaza Theater stands in the center with the Tower and Circle [Fountain Café] Buildings to the right.

The Changing of the Guard

Just as everything began to settle a bit from the flurry of post-War building and expansion, doctors at the Mayo Clinic diagnosed J.C. Nichols with cancer of the throat. Plaza manager Robert O'Keefe accompanied Nichols to Rochester, Mn. The doctors told O'Keefe the news first and asked how to break it to Nichols. O'Keefe responded that J.C. had always wanted news brought straight to him—good or bad. The doctors then told the developer that he had terminal cancer. Nichols' understandable inquiry was for an estimate of time left. The doctors gave him three months. This was in November 1949. J.C. Nichols died February 16, 1950—89 days after he left the Mayo Clinic.

The passing of the founder could have devastated the company and its activities—most particularly the Country Club Plaza. The shopping center had been almost an extension of his personality over the last 30 years of his life. Fortunately, Nichols left both the company and the Plaza in good hands.

J.C. Taylor, his first employee and long-time president of the company under J.C. Nichols' chairmanship, took over as Chairman of the Board. Nichols' older son, Miller, continued the direct family involvement by assuming the presidency. George Tourtellot continued to guide the Plaza for another eight years—all the while grooming Bob O'Keefe as his potential successor.

Nichols' funeral took place appropriately at Country Club Christian Church, in the heart of his Country Club District and just a few blocks from his home. Probably the most fitting tribute came from Kansas City Star editorial cartoonist Sam Ray. Appearing in the newspaper on the day of the funeral was a drawing of an empty chair looking out over a wonderful neighborhood. The legend simply said, "If you would see his epitaph, look around." The cartoon has been emblazoned in brass outside the main entrance to the J.C. Nichols Company on Ward Parkway.

It would be too much to say that J.C. Taylor and Miller Nichols took over without skipping a beat. Indeed, they were faced with a monumental task—replacing a legend. Not every action taken under their leadership—which lasted for 13 years—was exactly what J.C. Nichols would have done. At least, that's what their critics said. What is ultimately most important, however, is that the Nichols Company and the Country Club Plaza grew and prospered beyond the days of the founder. Few second-generation family-owned businesses in America can make that claim.

Dedication of the J.C. Nichols Memorial Fountain May 15, 1960

For almost a decade following the death of J.C. Nichols, Miller Nichols searched for an appropriate memorial to his memory.

Plaza Profile: J.C. Taylor

This son of Emporia, Ks. may have had the greatest difficulty taking leadership. For decades he had provided the conservative center for his mentor and friend, J.C. Nichols, who was always out there—thinking and doing and going. J.C. Taylor stayed home and minded the business. That was the role in which he was most comfortable. Leadership of the company in the absence of the elder Nichols was a fearful thing.

Yet, the testimony of employees and the record of the company in the 1950s and early '60s present a picture of growth and adaptation. Sometimes, he and Miller did not see eye-to-eye. For that matter, sometimes he and J.C. had disagreed as well. What they worked out was a method in which Taylor continued to run a conservative ship while Miller frequently sought out new opportunities for the company by means of viewing life from the masthead. This was a good combination—J.C. Taylor working with the Nichols—father, and then son. It kept the company solvent and strong while adapting and leading in the area of land development and retailing in the Kansas City region.

J.C. Taylor always lived a relatively quiet life. He served on his share of boards and in official positions with the Real Estate associations and such, but primarily he watched the direction of the company carefully. Allied with staunchly conservative company Treasurer, Frank Grant (the man who would check to see if pencils were down to the required two inches before allowing replacement), J.C. Taylor watched expenses while J.C. and Miller Nichols sought more income and opportunities. The company needed both approaches badly.

Plaza Symbolism: the Tower, the Light, and the Fountain

These three elements have figured in more photographs of the Country Club Plaza than any others. To out-of-town visitors, these features at 47th and J.C. Nichols Parkway are familiar images from various forms of advertising for Kansas City and the Plaza.

Plaza Profile: Miller Nichols

As the middle child among the Nichols children, Miller always sought to maintain his rightful place. With a strong older sister like Eleanor and a bright, happy younger brother like Clyde, Miller had his work cut out for him. That was true in another way as well. Because he was the older son, everyone, including himself, assumed he would succeed his father. Miller went to the University of Kansas, pledged Beta Theta Pi fraternity, and became something of a BMOC (Big Man On Campus) like his father before him.

Yet, Miller also did things a little differently from his father. He didn't become Phi Beta Kappa or manage an athletic team. Rather he pursued a well-rounded lifestyle for a young man at a Midwestern university in the late 1920s. In other words, while making no mistake about his heritage, Miller struck out on his own as well. This pattern of independence repeated itself when he took over the company presidency after his father's death in 1950.

Miller always believed in buying property ahead of its use. J.C. had certainly done that, but the older Nichols almost exclusively bought raw land far in advance of expecting to be able to use it. Miller more frequently bought property which had already advanced in its stage of development.

A prime example was in the 1950s when Miller wanted to buy houses across Brush Creek and west of Wornall Road for future Plaza expansion. J.C. Taylor was resistant. The company did not make the purchase, but the board allowed Miller to do it on his own. He did so, and these sites became the ultimate location for the Alameda Plaza Hotel (now Ritz-Carlton) and the Alameda towers condominiums nearby. Miller sold the land back to the company for what he had in it when the time was right for development.

Miller Nichols was persistent. In fact, that is the motto on his business card—"Persistence." Sometimes, people who want to do things differently from the way this younger Nichols wanted to do them resented that trait. Miller stuck to it when he thought he was right. With the company and the Plaza over the 38 years he presided over them, he was right much more than wrong.

Like his father, Miller Nichols made the Plaza an extension of himself. Even in the late 1990s, he continues to look for ways in which the Plaza can be made better. He continues to buy land north of the Plaza in the hopes that it will one day be useful either for expansion or protection of that valuable property. In the early 1990s, he personally paid for the construction of a new domed clock tower to serve as an information center on Kansas City and the Plaza at the intersection of Wornall and 47th Street. He did it because he believed it would improve the Plaza and help Kansas City.

Expansion Extends in the 1950s

The '50s decade proved to be a period of tremendous change at the Plaza and throughout Kansas City and the metropolitan region. The establishment of a branch store by Emery, Bird, Thayer at 47th and Broadway in 1949 probably signaled one aspect of the change more than anything else. As late as 1946, executives at that department store decried the coming of Sears to the Plaza as much as anyone else downtown. Then the Jones Store company established a branch at 31st and Troost. EBT did not want to miss an opportunity to defend their downtown position by constructing a flanking operation at the Plaza. EBT did well with its Plaza branch. In the early 1960s, EBT expanded it substantially, but by 1969, its downtown store closed and the Plaza branch sold to another competitor, Macy's.

In the mid-1950s, downtown fashion retailer Harzfeld's had the Nichols Company build a branch store for it at Nichols Road (renamed for J.C. after his death) and Pennsylvania. Office buildings and additional high-rise apartments appeared all around the Plaza during the 1950s. Sometimes the Nichols Company participated in the development; other times, as in the 1920s, Nichols sold land to other developers. Sometimes, developers obtained land and launched projects that merely fed off Plaza popularity. Regardless of the stimulus, the Plaza grew substantially during the decade.

Pomona Court, Broadway and Ward Parkway. 1972.

The Pomona Court provided one of the newest attractions on the Plaza in the early 1970s. The site served as a Standard Oil gasoline station from the Plaza's earliest days to the late 1960s. In a complicated land swap involving acreage worth more than $1 million on the open market, Miller Nichols got Standard Oil to agree to terminate their lease. These mini-skirted young women celebrated the "feel" of the newly created Plaza landmark.

Alameda Plaza Hotel. Winter 1972

Culminating a decade-long effort to acquire the land and construct the building, the Nichols Company opened the Alameda Plaza Hotel in 1972. The imposing curved structure challenges photographers in most seasons because of its close proximity to Brush Creek and the Plaza itself. In winter, the trees provide contrast rather than interference to the camera and the human eye. In the 1990s the hotel became the Ritz-Carlton.

For the daily resident or the occasional visitor, the Pomona Court at Broadway and Ward Parkway provides one of the most beautifully framed spots from which to view this marvelous piece of Plaza architecture.

A light fixture and street sign at Wyandotte and Nichols Road provide a different perspective of the Theater Tower.

Chapter 6: Let There Be Fountains, Towers and Lights

Architects speak of the "defining elements" of a structure as the aspects of appearance that make people remember it. The Plaza is an assemblage of structures and open space. Different defining elements affected shoppers and visitors over time. Since 1967, three constructions—a fountain, a tower and a light fixture—found their way into thousands of pictures of the picturesque setting.

The fountain appeared partially as a gift of the J.C. Nichols children to Kansas City, Mo. The J.C. Nichols Memorial Fountain with its heroic horse-born figures and flying sprays went in at the foot of Mill Creek Park, directly opposite the Suydam Building, first structure erected according to the Plaza plan in 1922-23. Dedication took place in May 1960. Ironically in some ways, this first defining element of the Plaza is not officially part of the privately owned space at all. The J.C. Nichols Fountain rests on public land under ownership of the Parks and Recreation Board.

One result of this distinction is that the Nichols Fountain frequently becomes the focal point of all types of public events. The Fountain then takes on a "town hall" type of role as a place for those wishing to exercise free-speech rights in defense of a cause.

This reality lends yet another layer of importance to the role of the Plaza in the Kansas City community consciousness. Because even television commentators confuse the publicly open park and Nichols Fountain with the Plaza itself, residents and visitors alike frequently conclude that political activities occur at the shopping center. It is another way in which the Plaza, or at least the Nichols Memorial Fountain—one of the great symbols of the Plaza—serves as more of a downtown center than the government buildings actually located in the civic center some 35 blocks north.

The tower and the light fixture made their appearance in 1967, some seven years after the J.C. Nichols Memorial Fountain began spewing forth its beauty. Called both the "Giralda Tower" and the "Seville Light" this tallest of all Plaza towers almost went up elsewhere in the shopping area some 28 years earlier. J.C. Nichols apparently saw the original tower for the first time on his trip to Spain in 1922. By 1929, he had Earl Allen of the architectural staff (and his future son-in-law) draw a rendering of how the tower would look at the south end of a proposed building along the west side of Broadway.

At the time, this location formed the west end of the Plaza. Had the tower actually been constructed on the proposed site, it would have ultimately served as the centerpiece of the shopping area rather than as the eastern entrance. Company records indicate that the decision not to build in 1929 was based on the perception that the tower was too tall for the surrounding buildings. As ultimately constructed in 1967, the base building appears in photos to be in roughly the same proportion as Allen rendered for the earlier site in 1929.

Another possibility seems almost as likely. The Knabe building on Broadway begun in late 1929, opened in 1930 after the onset of the Great Depression. Economic hard times may well have served to postpone the placement of this Plaza icon. The 1967 plans called for a tower built to exactly one-half the dimensions of the original Seville Cathedral Giralda Tower. In this way, the tower does seem to fit surrounding scale while still providing a visual focal point at the eastern entrance to the area.

In the original Earl Allen design, a cross topped the tower. For the Plaza of the 1960s, Miller Nichols and Company officials determined to have a copy made of the "statue of faith" which capped the Seville original. That first statue was set on a swivel to serve as a weather vane—the Spanish name for which is "giralda." As a result, in Seville the tower is often referred to as "the giralda tower." The Kansas City statue is permanently set to prevent weathering problems, yet the name, "Giralda" in capitalized form, is retained. Earl Allen indicated his awareness of the name in his 1929 drawing—one of the storefronts (not built as drawn) indicated a movie theater entrance with the name "Giralda" as the marquee. Both the statue of faith atop the tower and the metal portions of the light fixture came from the studios of sculptor Bernhard Zuckerman.

Miller Nichols spotted the light fixture on its small fountain base when he visited Seville with his family in the mid-1960s. The original light fixture stands in an open square ("plaza" in Spanish). He even had Nichols Company president Davis Jackson come to Spain to look at both the tower and light in their original setting. The two agreed that both were necessary to provide the proper effect in Kansas City. Dedication of the light took place in October 1967.

As the Christmas lights lit the night sky in November 1967, one might say the stage was finally set for a way to recall the Plaza. The J.C. Nichols Fountain spurted, the Seville light flickered, and the Giralda Tower shone in brilliant white outline form. It is the picture of the Plaza as most have remembered it ever since.

Because of scenes like the Fountain, Tower, and Light, many Kansas Citians feel so much personal ownership of the privately controlled Plaza as an institution. Understandably therefore, changes on the Plaza are almost always met with skepticism and concern. Just as the additions of these icons demonstrate, the Plaza has been changing from its earliest days.

Changes came in the form of people as well. In 1958, George Tourtellot had to phase down his activity because of ill health. While continuing to serve as company vice-president for commercial properties until 1963, he turned over day-to-day operations to Robert O'Keefe who had worked for the company since 1932, with time out for World War II service.

J.C. Taylor retired as Chairman of the Board in 1963, causing a shake-up at the very top. Miller Nichols had served his apprenticeship under his father, and had been company president since 1950. Though of different generations and sometimes different temperament, the two had worked together well over the decade-plus since the passing of the first J.C.—Mr. Nichols.

Miller became Chairman of the Board in the new regime after 1963. A man of almost equal age whom he met during naval service in World War II, Davis K. Jackson assumed the presidency.

As envisioned in the early 1920s by J.C. Nichols, the land around the Plaza sprouted new apartment buildings in almost every direction during the 1960s. The Nichols Company participated in building two of the largest such structures—Regency House and the Sulgrave Apartments on 49th Street south of the Loma Vista to Villa Serena row along Brush Creek. Their partner in this construction was City Bond and Mortgage Company of Kansas. Fred Brady, J.C. Taylor's son-in-law and father of 1990s Nichols Company president Barrett Brady, was a vice-president of the firm. Fred Brady also long sat on the Nichols Company Board by virtue of stock given him and his wife by Taylor.

Other large buildings constructed around the Plaza in this period included the John Hancock building (now First Business Bank of Kansas City, 47th & Madison); Winston Churchill Apartments, 48th & Summit; Sunset Towers, Ward Parkway & Roanoke; Parkway Towers, north on Nichols Parkway; and Oak Hall Apartments, east on Warwick Boulevard. Even more residents came to depend on the Plaza for primary shopping during this period.

In almost all cases, this new construction replaced earlier lower density housing. Some of the buildings took the place of former small apartment structures; others were built on the site of two or three single family houses or duplexes.

The first case of tearing down an existing Plaza building came in August,

1961. The Chandler building served that floral company well from its remodeling in 1920 to 1958. After moving its business south, the family leased the building to another florist for a couple of years. Then in 1961, Mrs. Chandler decided the time had come to sell the building and land to the Company.

Miller Nichols had been waiting for this day for a long time. Neither he nor the other Company leaders had any specific idea how immediately to use the site, but the building was razed in August, 1961. Initially, the land provided additional parking for nearby establishments. In June 1966, the Nichols Company announced plans for the construction of a much enlarged space for Swanson's fashion store with the Giralda Tower placed at its northeast corner.

The enlargement of Swanson's, combined with the construction in 1964-65, gave notice that the Plaza was becoming even more fashion-conscious. Upscale stores such as Jack Henry, Woolf Brothers, and the smaller previous Swanson's site had gradually increased their presences, but the new, larger structures opening in 1965-67 served notice that fashion merchandising took center stage. Admittedly, Hall's emphasized fine china, crystal and silver even more than clothing. What was not well publicized at the time was that the Hall family had the controlling interest in Swanson's as well as the Hall's store.

Swanson's fashion store took up residency on the Plaza in 1941 in the then-new 110 Ward Parkway building (now the KC Masterpiece Barbeque Restaurant). Mrs. Maude Springe operated it with nieces Kathryn R. Meyer and Helen R. Schaefer, building it into a major enterprise during the 1950s. As a backdrop for the planned tower, the Nichols Company constructed a two story building in distinctive Spanish architecture and décor. Some of the buildings put up in the 1950s such as

Harzfeld's and the Neptune building (today's Houston's Restaurant and Abercrombie and Fitch) were assemblages of concrete block and slump brick which retained only a hint of southwestern influence. Swanson's would be built in the more recognizable styles of earlier years.

One type of change took place only gradually. Among the first revenue-producing locations on the Plaza, gasoline stations gradually gave way to other uses. Possibly the most spectacular example of such a change occurred in the late 1960s. A Standard Oil (now Amoco) station stood at the northeast intersection of Broadway and Ward Parkway since before the Mill Creek Building went up.

Miller Nichols determined that he wanted something more distinctive than a gasoline station gracing the west end of the J.C. Nichols Company building on Ward Parkway. When Bob O'Keefe approached Standard officials about the possibility of ending their profitable lease, he discovered they would be happy to do so—for a price. According to company records, obtaining the rights to the corner cost the company over $1,000,000. Additionally, the company had to put up three new stations for the petroleum concern elsewhere in the city.

After all that, a decision about how to beautify the corner had to be made. Not surprisingly, the result was a fountain. But this was not to be just any fountain. In the center rose the mythical figure of Pomona, goddess of vineyards and orchards. From her feet and over the lip of the bowl from which she rose ran an unbroken stream of water, powered by a powerful pump hidden below. The result is probably one of the most photographed locations on the Plaza. Professionals and Kodak-toting grandmothers alike seem drawn to the site, for many years an entrance to

Woolf Brothers. This little corner and the expensive story of how it came to be are just a part of what makes the Plaza what it is.

The trend for stores originally operating only in Downtown locations to expand or relocate to the Plaza increased during the 1960s. Hall's served as one prime example. Emery, Bird, Thayer enjoyed a Plaza presence from 1949; in 1960 it more than doubled the size of its Plaza location on the northwest corner of 47th and Broadway.

The move to the Plaza that generated the most controversy during the 1960s involved the J.C. Nichols Company and the Kansas City Board of Trade. The latter institution dated back to the 1870s as a grain trading organization. Since the 1880s, it has served as the only commodity exchange in the United States exchanging futures contracts on "hard red winter wheat"—the premier bread wheat planted on the Great Plains of Kansas and elsewhere.

From its inception as a financial institution, the Board occupied part or all of a Downtown office building. As necessary, they moved to larger quarters within the Downtown area. In the early 1960s, members of the exchange sought larger quarters once again. When all efforts at locating or even building such in a Downtown location fell through, Board officers discussed the possibility of relocating to a site owned by the Nichols Company on Main Street just south of the Plaza.

Viewed at the time as a blow to the prestige of the downtown office infrastructure, the move of the influential Board of Trade to the Plaza in 1965 served as a wake-up call to Downtown advocates. These bankers, attorneys, and business people have since worked long and hard to keep the major offices of business and professional entities centered in their district. In an age when decentralization far beyond the reaches of the

Plaza is commonplace, the major banks, many of the larger legal firms, and significant numbers of other professional organizations continue to office in Downtown locations or near the Country Club Plaza.

Restaurants have served as important gathering places and revenue producers throughout the history of the Plaza. Hunter Brothers Drug Store in the original Suydam (Mill Creek) building provided the first opportunity for prepared food on the Plaza at their luncheonette. Many others followed.

The 210 West 47th Street address was connected with food from the beginning. Piggly Wiggly opened its first Plaza store there in 1923. Other, non-food-related stores followed, but in 1933 the Plaza celebrated the end of Prohibition with the opening of Clare Martin's Plaza Tavern. A young man who grew up in the food service business in Kansas City bought the lease in 1946 after his war service ended. He was Jud Putsch who remodeled the site and reopened it as "Putsch's 210." For over 40 years this mainstay symbolized fine dining on the Plaza.

Jud and Virginia Putsch opened a cafeteria on the Plaza less than a half block away from Putsch's 210 in 1953. It evolved into the most successful cafeteria operation on the Plaza for decades. The Nichols Company built a little structure at the west end of their 47th Street parking station, remodeling it into a layered open and enclosed structure in 1959. Jud Putsch took the lease and created the long-popular Putsch's Coffee House at 47th and Broadway. (Sharper Image now occupies the build-

ing). A few years later, the Nichols company opened up some basement space for him to establish Putsch's Side Door cocktail lounge with its entrance off Broadway. The very popular Putsch's Sidewalk Café opened in 1967 just as the Giralda Tower and Seville Light (along with Swanson's) took shape a little more than a block to the east. The Putschs retired in 1971 shortly after they celebrated their 25th year of operations on the Plaza. Montgomery Ward stores bought and operated the restaurants initially.

Other changes took place on the Plaza during these years. In 1961, Rothschild's expanded its location at Central and 47th Street so that it could add the women's lines it already carried at its Downtown location. Sears expanded its auto service area by purchasing an adjacent gasoline station; the company also constructed the three-tier parking garage on the west side of Jefferson at the west end of Nichols Road in 1963.

An event of national and international significance partially took place on the Plaza in January 1963. Former Mexican President Jose Aleman returned to Kansas City for a People-to-People event sponsored by Hall's founder, Joyce Hall. At this event, former U.S. Presidents Harry Truman and Dwight Eisenhower met and visited cordially for the first time since Truman had relinquished the White House a decade prior. During the festivities, Aleman returned to the Plaza court named in his honor. Plaza officials unveiled a new tile mural entitled "Panorama of the Americas" in his presence to further distinguish the site.

During this period the Nichols Company embarked on what would become the focus of the next stage of Plaza development—the Alameda Plaza Hotel. They began proceedings to get zoning changed to allow hotel construction on the south side of Brush Creek at Wornall and Ward Parkway. This proved to be an extended effort which went all the way up the Missouri Court system. Finally, in 1967, the Company won a definitive judgment in court and proceeded with plans for the hotel.

The Plaza Bank of Commerce announced it was remodeling part of the property it purchased at 46th Terrace and Wyandotte into a motor bank facility. Two more Plaza neighbors appeared adjacent to the shopping area. Mid-Continent Bank opened facilities in a new office building constructed on Main Street across the corner from the Board of Trade site. Directly east of the Board of Trade, the Kansas City School Board erected the Plaza Branch Library. Both these facilities opened in 1967.

Some stores enlarged—others came and went—the symbols of the Plaza became the triple focus of the J.C. Nichols Fountain, the Giralda Tower, and the Seville Light. Change was constant, and yet, the 1960s served as the era in which many Kansas Citians anchor their sense of what the Plaza is in the 1990s and beyond. Very possibly some of the reason for the somewhat nostalgic view of the early to mid-1960s as the "heyday" of the Plaza lies in the events which followed closely after.

The Theater Tower stands out even more brilliantly when framed against either the dark American Century office buildings or the bright blue Kansas City sky.

Dome of Parkway 600 Restaurant against backdrop of Sheraton Suites [high-rise] and 6th Church of Christ, Scientist.

Plaza Feature: Fountains

Of course, one of the great symbols of the entire shopping district is the J.C. Nichols Memorial Fountain located in Mill Creek Park at the east entrance. In fact there has long been a fountain in that general entry area. The first fountain on the Plaza was given by the J.C. Nichols Company to Kansas City back in 1923. It was a rather small fountain, just large enough for small children to peek over its lip to see the pool of water. That original fountain is now replaced by the one integrated into the base of the Seville Light standing before the great Giralda Tower at 47th Street and Nichols Parkway.

One of the most poignant fountains is a small piece on Nichols Road dedicated to the memory of Eleanor and Earl Allen, sister and brother-in-law to Miller and Clyde Nichols. They died together in a tragic housefire of undetermined origin in 1961. Earl Allen contributed much to the beauty of the Plaza over his decades of employment in the architectural department of the Nichols Company.

Other fountains include the Neptune Fountain, the Fountain of Bacchus in Chandler Court near the Cheesecake Factory restaurant, the Pool of the Four Fauns, the Mermaid Pool, the Pomona Fountain near Eddie Bauer's and Diana and the Waterfall in front of the Ritz-Carlton.

Kansas City is known as the City of Fountains. Nowhere else in Kansas City is this more true than on the Country Club Plaza.

Fountains

Kansas City is the City of Fountains. Nowhere in the City of Fountains will you find as many examples as in the Country Club Plaza. The J.C. Nichols Memorial Fountain.

Fountain face [Seville Light, 47th & J.C. Nichols Parkway]

Fountain of Diana [Ritz-Carlton Hotel].

Fountain of Bacchus [Chandler Court].

Pomona Fountain [Pomona Court]; Neptune Fountain [Balcony Building].

The Ritz-Carlton Hotel provides Plaza visitors with five-star accomadations.

Chapter 7:
The Place You Have to Go

FROM ITS EARLIEST days, J.C. Nichols intended for the Plaza to attract out-of-town visitors. He even planned to build a hotel on the site that ultimately became home to the Kansas City Board of Trade. Footings and foundations for such a structure lay in place for decades behind some small stores facing Main Street in the 4800 block. The time and money simply never coincided for the developer on that project.

Miller Nichols never forgot about the possibility, however. During the late 1950s and early '60s he quietly negotiated with Dr. Ernest D. Fear who had previously assembled an impressive number of duplexes and single family homes under his ownership. Fear died in Kansas City in 1963. Nichols then had to deal with Fear's estate. He thought they had worked out a suitable deal to acquire sufficient land for a 300-room hotel and four or five additional high rise luxury apartments similar to those in the recently completed Regency House across Wornall Road.

To accomplish the goal, a change in the neighborhood zoning was necessary. The Company went through the proper channels. Opposition surfaced in the form of neighborhood residents who opposed the idea of high-rise apartments and a busy hotel "in their backyard," as they viewed it. Initially, judges ruled in favor of the protestors; the Nichols Company kept appealing such verdicts. Four years after requesting the zoning change, Miller Nichols and his Company gained approval for the zoning change in the Missouri State Supreme Court. It is not accidental that Miller Nichols claims "Persistence" is his middle name (actually, Miller Nichols has no official middle name or initial—a rarity in American society these days).

The Alameda Plaza and its successor, the Ritz-Carlton, provided the Plaza area with its first on-site, first-class hotel accommodations. This brought in convention visitors and vacationers eager to shop the Plaza stores and to sample the abundant nightlife. From its opening in 1972 to the present, the hotel south of Brush Creek has reinforced the Country Club Plaza as one of the premier shopping destinations in the United States.

An additional step toward creation of destination accommodations on the Plaza came in 1975 with the opening of the Raphael Hotel at Wornall and Ward Parkway. Located directly across the street from the Alameda Plaza, the Raphael was built in the late 1920s as part of the McCandless high-rise apartment boom across Brush Creek from the Plaza. Prior to conversion to hotel status, the Raphael served 45 years as

Shoppers enjoy a sunny stroll through the Plaza.

the Villa Serena Apartments. This conversion of the Villa Serena from residential to transient hotel status signifies at least one aspect of the transition of the Plaza into more of a destination shopping location.

The hotel was important in this quest, but other factors came into play as well. For much of America, shopping has existed largely as a necessary evil during the lives of most citizens. By the late 1960s, however, there existed a growing number of persons who wished for entertainment while they shopped for things they wanted more than for what they needed. In that respect, the Plaza was in the right place at the right time.

Going to the Plaza always fell, at least partially, into the entertainment category because of all the decoration, sculpture, and creative architecture. Live music in the taverns and clubs as well as out on the sidewalks helped boost this entertainment aspect. Now the Plaza Motor Inn and the Alameda Plaza provided places for people to stay even longer to shop "on the Plaza."

Other forces brought greater change to the Plaza. One of Kansas City's oldest retailing institutions, Emery, Bird, Thayer, was deemed by its conglomerate owner during the summer of 1968 to be unable to stay in business. While EBT had a branch on the Plaza as early as 1949, it did not expand to other suburban areas in any significant way. No one stepped forward to take over the Downtown location (ultimately destroyed to make room for United Missouri Bank), but Macy's agreed to take over the Plaza and Independence branches.

Nothing in EBT's loss indicated weakness in the Plaza market, but it definitely signaled a decline in demand for centralized shopping facilities

downtown. Actually, the EBT store on the Plaza expanded substantially in 1962, more than doubling its retail space at the site. For that reason, it was an attractive takeover location for Macy's, which had never previously had a Plaza location.

In 1972, a major change occurred on the restaurant scene. Gilbert Robinson opened Houlihan's Old Place next door to its popular Plaza III location on Pennsylvania. The name came from the previous occupant of the site, Tom Houlihan's Men's Wear. This shift put Gilbert Robinson into the same category as Putsch's. Both operated quite successful restaurant locations adjacent to each other. The key in each case was to target a somewhat different clientele through menu selection and décor. The Houlihan's concept proved so popular that it survived the breakup of Gilbert Robinson in the 1980s and provided the name for one of the successor companies.

A signal of the subtle changes taking place came in 1974 when Wally Westphal closed his Plaza Hair Cut Shop on Jefferson after operating it in that location for almost 30 years. The Plaza moved away from service-oriented businesses, which generated only limited rents, toward food and fashion retailers who offered higher volume sales and higher percentage rents to the Company.

From its earliest days, the J.C. Nichols Company operated the Plaza and its other shopping areas on a percentage rent basis. In the beginning, this meant they would probably not get rent income for space comparable to that generated in more densely shopped areas such as Downtown or at streetcar transfer points. The percentage-rent arrangement helped secure tenants in the early years. It also did something else—it made the Nichols Company a partner with every merchant on the Plaza. As sales

Out to lunch.

increased, so did the rent and the profits to the Company. If sales leveled off or declined, rental income to the Company likewise fell.

One of the biggest changes came in 1974 when Sears announced it was closing its Plaza location. At the time, this seemed to point to terrific problems ahead for the Plaza, because, as the saying went, "If Sears can't make at the Plaza, who can?" As things turned out, both Sears and the Plaza survived, although there has been almost more change at Sears than at the shopping center. Indeed, what was not apparent to outsiders in 1974 was that Sears did have serious problems as a retailer which would take the better part of two decades both to become apparent and to be addressed.

Regardless of the reasons for Sears' exit, it left a big hole in the west end of the retailing area. The first thing the Nichols Company did was to buy the land and building from Sears. (Sears continued to operate its auto service and appliance retailing center until 1978). After a good deal of study, the concept of Seville Square became public in January 1975. This enclosed shopping center within the Plaza opened its first stores in February 1977.

One of the most stable and profitable stores in Seville Square has been its ground level corner McDonald's Restaurant. The location has kept a constant flow of customers satisfied for over 20 years. It even sports its own piece of Plaza statuary—a boy eating a hamburger and reading a book. Entitled "Out to Lunch," it appropriately graces the sidewalk near the outside entrance to the store.

Very possibly the most memorable event in the entire history of Plaza began to unfold on September 12, 1977. A low pressure cell concentrated such intense rainfall in the immediate region that Kansas City recorded an all-time record of over 11 inches in one 24-hour period.

Floods are not unusual in Kansas City history. Big ones did significant damage in 1903, 1951, and 1993. In all those cases, the flooding was in the Kansas and Missouri River valleys, dozens of blocks north and west of Brush Creek and the Plaza. In September 1977, the problem had little to do with the big rivers; the intense rainfall centered in the Brush Creek and Blue River watersheds. So much rain filled the Blue River that it could not empty water fast enough into the Missouri. The backup then caused a similar problem on Brush Creek.

Since the 1930s and the days of Tom Pendergast, Brush Creek ran over a concrete apron with a little irrigation ditch-sized trough carrying the normal flow quickly away. Even when sizeable rains fell, the straightness of the channel and the concrete apron usually moved even high waters quickly away from the Plaza district.

When the Blue River proved unable to handle its own high flow and that of Brush Creek, both streams began to back up rapidly. Suddenly the man-made channel for Brush Creek became a liability rather than an asset. The backed-up stream flowed up and out of its rather narrow banks onto Ward Parkway and into the stores in the lowest parts of the Plaza. Below-ground parking garages and storage basements in stores flooded almost instantaneously. Ultimately water entered most establishments on the south side of Nichols road and all facing Ward Parkway. Even a few businesses on the north side of Nichols Road suffered water at low levels entering their ground floors and flooding basement areas.

When waters receded, 25 lives had been lost throughout the metro area. The devastation on the Plaza was huge. Automobiles had been strewn about along Ward Parkway and in parking garages as though they were toys. Layers of mud and muck filled lower levels and covered merchandise and fixtures. Almost half the 155 Plaza businesses received flood

Damage caused by the 1977 Plaza flood.

The Place You Have to Go

damage. Hall's Plaza store sustained damage to its structural integrity as well as to merchandise and décor.

It couldn't have come at a worse time. As any retailer will relate, the fall selling season is the most important of the year. Christmas sales ring up from October through December. Many of the stores had just received their entire Christmas inventory and were waiting to begin putting it on display. Losses were totaled in the millions across the Plaza.

Amazingly, through hard work and dedication by Plaza merchants and employees of the J.C. Nichols Company, the vast majority of the flooded businesses reopened by December 1, 1977. Even more surprising, the Plaza Art Fair, scheduled for just ten days after the flood took place, went on as scheduled in the parts of the Plaza not flooded. Hall's and the Nichols company embarked on an extensive renovation and expansion which resulted in the addition of another display floor and more parking levels as part of the Hall's building. Only two tenants canceled leases while four new businesses opened on the Plaza in the pre-Christmas run-up season.

The Nichols Company spent well over $2,000,000 helping to repair the damage. The city of Kansas City, Mo., spent hundreds of thousands of additional dollars to repair streets, sewers, water lines, and Brush Creek itself in the immediate Plaza area alone. By 1996, an entirely new and deeper Brush Creek channel emerged hopefully to prevent any recurrence of what in Kansas City is referred to as "the Plaza Flood of 1977."

Houlihan's is a popular destination among Plaza visitors.

Plaza Profile: Merchants Make the Difference

The Plaza is more than the sum of its parts. The atmosphere, the excitement, and the delight all derive from the experiences shoppers have with merchants and each other.

The first four women who opened stores on the Plaza in 1923 all had prior experience in their type of store or service. What they provided in the new setting was the beginning of the Plaza feeling that grew with the addition of Wolferman's "Good Things to Eat" store, the Suydam Decorating Company, and even Hunter Brothers Drug Store.

Some merchants such as Woolf Brothers and Rothchilds came to the Plaza after years of operating elsewhere in the city. When they closed their Plaza stores, they closed all the other locations they operated in this area as well. The reason these stores, and others like Swanson's, Mindlin's, and Chasnoff's stayed so long on the Plaza was that they had a faithful clientele that came back month after month or year after year.

A whole host of companies came and went during the Plaza's first 75 years. Some of the original leaseholders in 1923 lasted but a few years, however, many operated for extended periods; Mrs. Mary McGavran went on to operate Plaza beauty salons into the 1960s. Several of the owners retired from their businesses on the Plaza, sometimes closing them at the time, other times selling them to employees or interested buyers. In the majority of cases, the businesses ended because either what they sold or the way in which they dispensed their goods or services changed in public acceptance.

The point is that the bulk of the businesses no longer operating on the Plaza left for reasons inherent to the particular situation of the owner(s) or the industry of which they were a part. Additionally, economic conditions have swung wildly at times. The Plaza did weather the Great Depression, after all.

The friendly sidewalk atmosphere of the Plaza.

Plaza Feature: Statuary

One of the things that has always made the Plaza, "The Plaza," is the distinctive statuary one finds simply strolling along the streets or around a corner. Some have compared the Plaza to an outdoor sculpture gallery. In certain ways, it meets those expectations.

Early during J.C. Nichols' development days, reporters visiting Kansas City from other places around the country and the world asked him why he put pieces of statuary at intersections throughout his residential sections or at significant points throughout the Plaza and his other shopping districts. His reply was telling. He explained that each piece of sculpture or statuary created a certain sense of interest and value in the mind of potential residents and shoppers. It meant something special to them to be where they were. In that frame of mind, they made better residents and better shoppers. In other words, the art had a definite business value.

The same concept holds true on the Plaza in the 1990s as it did in the 1920s. If people find details they can delight in, they will come back time and again. When they return, they will probably buy goods or services that are available in the surrounding stores and shops. When people feel good, they will buy. It all goes back to that sense that shopping has its entertainment value as well as its economic purpose.

Some pieces of art work or sculpture have generated more interest over the years than others. Among the most popular are "The Sleeping Child" at 47th Street and Broadway. This small figure lying in silent repose affects many passers-by quite deeply. One Plaza resident even covers the naked figure on cold winter nights—according to one Plaza legend. The Company first placed this figure in 1963. That statuary was destroyed by an auto accident in the early 1990s. Miller Nichols personally paid for a new sculpture of the figure in its original Carrara marble form. The new sculpture was placed in 1996.

Children particularly seem to love to rub the nose of the Bronze Boar on 47th Street. Coins dropped in its base are thought to bring good luck and are contributed to Children's Mercy Hospital.

Another Plaza favorite is the representation of Sir Winston and Lady Churchill placed in 1984 on the rebuilt Broadway Bridge over Brush Creek between the Plaza and the Ritz-Carlton/Raphael Hotel locations. This bronze piece is entitled "Married Love" and depicts Lady Churchill looking toward the former Prime Minister who is himself depicted looking off into the distance. Churchill himself commissioned the original small bronze piece on which the larger work was based.

At the west end of the Plaza on Jefferson Street, next to the Gap for Kids, a bronze of Benjamin Franklin sits reading a paper on a park bench. Young children often like to have their pictures taken next to this depiction of one of America's founding fathers. The Franklin piece is a relatively new addition to the Plaza; the Miller Nichols family donated it in 1990.

Statuary

If one wishes to gain a bit of a classical education in the myths of the Greeks and Romans, Plaza statuary can provide some wonderful opportunities. Among the figures depicted in stone or bronze are Bacchus, god of revelry; Neptune, god of the sea; Pomona, goddess of vineyards and orchards; Diana, goddess of the moon, Mercury, god of trade and travel; Pegasus, the winged horse of victory; as well as fauns, mermaids, nymphs, satyrs, and other figures of classical mythology.

Religious figures come in for frequent representation, as well, with the inclusion of a Madonna and Child and the Old Testament character, Ruth. To those familiar with Spanish and Latin American architecture, the various domes and towers of the Plaza are reminiscent of churches and cathedrals throughout those lands. Nowhere, of course, is this more evident than in the Giralda Tower and Seville Light which are replicas of what can be seen from the plaza in front of the Seville Cathedral in Spain.

Native America receives attention in a number of popular art works: the statue of Massasoit stands guard at Main and 47th Streets, a mural of enamel on porcelain entitled "Panorama of the Americas" illustrates a wall in Aleman Court; while the "Indian Ceremonial Buffalo Dance" bronze bas-relief represents traditional dances at Taos Pueblo in New Mexico.

No other shopping area in the world contains the variety and quality of original and replicated statuary and sculpture represented in fountains, on walkways, and in little niches scattered throughout the Country Club Plaza.

On the Plaza, statuary creates a fantasy land of historical and mythical characters.

"Quiet Talk" between Mother and Child in a small niche of the Balcony Building on 47th St. near Broadway.

"Boy with a Thorn" attempts to extract the nuisance in front of the Raphael Hotel at Ward Parkway and Wornall Rd.

Cherubs play with sea creatures in the J.C. Nichols Fountain.

Heroic horses bear their native riders to battle against the sea creatures in the J.C. Nichols Fountain.

"Boy With Fish" median of 47th Street at J.C. Nichols Parkway near the Fountain Cafe; "Morning Prayer" depicts a small girl in prayer inside the watery streams of the Mermaid Fountain outside Eddie Bauer's at Broadway and Nichols Rd.

"Roman Sarcophagus" on the west wall of The Great Train Store, near Broadway & Nichols Rd.

Court of the Penguins, Pennsylvania & Nichols Rd.

"Massasoit" at 47th & Main near Winstead's.

The Wild Boar in front of the Balcony Building beckons to children to rub his nose and leave a coin for those at Children's Mercy Hospital.

"Mairried Love" [Broadway Bridge across from the Ritz-Carlton] portrays Winston and Lady Churchill in a relaxed moment on their English country manor.

"Sleeping Child" in the median of 47th Street at Broadway reminds us of the untroubled sleep of innocent childhood.

"The Invincible Spirit" of an American bald eagle stands guard along the sidewalk on Nichols Rd.

"Monkey Business" [Pomona Court] depicts an organ grinder much like the one who entertained Plaza shoppers for many years; "Pegasus," the mythical winged horse of victory, watches proudly from his place at Broadway and Nichols Rd.

The Plaza, First and Always

Chapter 8:
Plaza Destinations and More

THE PLAZA WOULD never quite be the same after the 1977 flood. But then, it is never quite the same one year from another. Some of the changes announced after the flood: The One Ward Parkway office building would be built on the former site of Sidney's Drive-In at Ward Parkway and Main. The Plaza Bowl, Woolworth's, Embassy II Theaters, and Muehlbach's Thriftway Grocery learned that their leases on Nichols Road opposite Harzfeld's would not be renewed. Rothchild's announced the closing of all its Kansas City stores, including its Plaza location and the Plaza Post Office site closed in November of that year. In their own way, each of these announcements ended an era.

The new office building at Main & Ward Parkway was to be built atop a three-story parking structure. This gave some breathing room to the Board of Trade immediately to the south. It also signaled the onset of even more office building construction all around the Plaza location during the 1980s.

Woolworth's proved to be a victim of the changing retail climate. While it had planned to continue its location on the Plaza, the company closed its downtown Kansas City store in 1965. By the late 1970s it was seeking to compete with the likes of K-Mart and Wal-Mart with its own line of Woolco stores. Nothing seemed to work well, and the one-time king of the "5 and dime" stores gradually disappeared from the scene all over America. Its exit from the Plaza came only slightly ahead of its disappearance elsewhere.

The public did not necessarily understand or agree with these changing trends in retailing. The non-renewal for Woolworth's drew loud complaints in the *Kansas City Star* and in other media. Without even knowing that the spot would be filled by Sak's Fifth Avenue, dozens of letter writers and hundreds of talk-show respondents condemned the Nichols management for its shortsightedness about the needs of the neighborhood around the Plaza.

The letter writers and callers were aware that the movie theaters and the long popular Plaza Bowl were leaving as well. The departure of the Post Office only intensified the complaints.

Inside the Nichols Company, several decisions motivated the actions. To a greater extent than ever, Company management recognized it was in a battle with the growing suburban malls for the consumer dollar. Malls organized around one or more "anchor stores" which were intended to draw large numbers of shoppers. The expectation was that the "anchors" brought

Plaza Art Fair enthusiasts mingle among the booths at the 1995 event.

shoppers who then bought goods at other smaller and less-well-advertised stores on the mall.

Using this philosophy, it is easy to see that Fred Wolferman's Plaza store served as the first anchor for the Plaza. The coming of Sears after World War II actually introduced the concept to outlying shopping areas in Kansas City. The arrival of Hall's and the expansion of Swanson's in the 1960s certainly added sizeable drawing stores to the Plaza mix.

By the late 1970s, however, Sears was gone, and the Plaza seemed to need a distinctive new

anchor to retain its shopping pre-eminence in the region. It also seemed important that the main Plaza anchor store(s) be as unique as possible. "Saks Fifth Avenue"—the very name exuded upscale trendiness around 1970. Certainly no mere mall in Kansas City could hope to attract such an instantly recognizable name in the retailing world.

In order to attract such a store, the Nichols Company knew it had to provide a large amount of space. This need for a unique anchor led to contacts with the parent company of Saks. Negotiations went on over some years. The Plaza Bowl moved in 1978; Woolworth's continued until its lease ended on December 31, 1980. The announcement that Saks would lease at the Plaza came shortly before Woolworth's closed its doors. Shortly before that time, Brooks Brothers, another nationally known men's clothing retailer announced it would take the former Muehlbach's Grocery space. Another new era on the Plaza began.

Muehlbach's did not leave the Plaza at that time, it simply moved to a somewhat smaller location on Jefferson Street on the west end of the shopping area. This set of buildings was one of the last large pieces of property repurchased by the Nichols Company. In the 1920s, J.C. Nichols sold the land between 48th and Ward Parkway, Pennsylvania to Jefferson to apartment builder C.E. Phillips. Phillips previously construct-

ed the "poet apartments" (i.e. the James Russell Lowell, the Carlyle, and the like) just west of Jefferson. The intervening Depression prevented any additional apartments at the time.

After World War II, a series of owners constructed commercial buildings which did not really conform to Plaza styles. The Nichols Company helped rent some of them, but never had control until 1966 when it traded land with the Shawnee Mission Medical Center and Plaza Savings in a complicated 3-way swap. Plaza Savings underwent several ownership changes to become Roosevelt Bank in the middle 1990s.

The removal of the Muehlbach-Woolworth building to make room for the Saks Fifth Avenue structure marked the second large tear-down of existing Plaza buildings. The first had been the Chandler building removal which ultimately became the Giralda Tower/Swanson's site. This visual change made the transition from Woolworth's to Saks even more noticeable to the general public. Over time, adjustment to the changes grew. Kansas Citians, suburbanites and visitors all developed an acceptance of the national retailing newcomers to the Plaza.

Across the corner from the Woolworth's/Saks site, the Sears Auto and Appliance Center continued a presence for that company on the Plaza after the main store closed in 1974. During the summer of 1978, Sears decided to abandon the auto service facilities as well. The Nichols Company moved quickly to purchase the property. With that purchase, Miller Nichols realized a level of control over Plaza property greater than any ever enjoyed by his father. Only the Skelley Office Building and the Plaza (now Commerce) bank locations remained outside the ownership of the Company in the main Plaza sections.

Within months of the purchase of the Sears Auto buildings, the Company announced plans for "the Court of the Penguins." This amounted to a series of boutiques facing an open court with a fountain and little penguin statuary frolicking about for atmosphere. Initially, Gucci opened a store on one end of the Court while DuVall's leased the large west-end building—formerly Sears Appliance Center.

For the buying public, these well-publicized changes in Plaza occupancy symbolized the "upscaling" of shopping at the Plaza. Ironically, for many long-time Plaza patrons, the opposite seemed to be the case. By the 1970s, fewer and fewer Plaza customers felt compelled to "dress up" to go shopping there.

The decade of the 1980s witnessed even greater change in the surrounding neighborhood than on the Plaza itself. Apartment buildings, office buildings, and condominium structures seemed to crop up overnight.

More than the departure of Woolworth's and the coming of Saks Fifth Avenue, the construction of ever more dense office and residential space around the Plaza in the 1980s changed the type of customer at the doors of its retail establishments. Huge construction projects, usually not involving the Nichols Company directly, made the Plaza area a destination for more people on a daily basis. A greater number of people lived and worked on or near the Plaza than at any previous time. This meant that more people came to shop during the noon hour or after 5:00 p.m. It also meant that Plaza restaurants potentially had greater numbers of noon and evening diners.

Project names took on pictuesque qualities—Plaza West, Plaza Steppes, Fountain View, and Sailors—to mention a few. The Sailors project carried with it the potential of changing the landscape east of the Plaza to a tremendous extent. At one point in its evolution, Sailors developers (some of whom were named "Sailors" and none of whom worked for the Nichols Company) projected a 56-story office building overlooking the

Plaza from behind Winstead's Restaurant on 47th Street. The potential impact of the structure and the number of workers it would have housed is mind-boggling. As it turned out, this particular project phased down as the excesses of the 1980s fell into the recession at the end of the decade. Now called Park Central Plaza, the residential apartment phase is getting underway.

The Twentieth Century Towers (now American Century) constructed at 46th and Main on a hill overlooking the Plaza above J.C. Nichols Fountain did have something of the effect projected by the Sailors proposal. Constructed in the late 1980s and early '90s, these two office buildings house the rapidly growing mutual funds company for which they are named. Over 1,000 report for work daily inside the twin dark-brown skyscrapers rising high over their parking garage base structures cascading down the hill to the edge of Mill Creek Park.

Similar kinds of changes west of Pennsylvania on 47th Street bring hundreds of people to the Plaza to work each week. In the mid-1990s even more projects of this type reached the City Planning Board of Kansas City government. The trend has yet to abate.

In addition to the rise of office towers, the 1980s and '90s witnessed the construction of more hotel space in the immediate Plaza vicinity. At the end of the 1970s, the Hilton Plaza Inn, the Alameda Plaza, and the Raphael accounted for all the hotel space within easy walking distance of the shopping area. Between 1980 and 1996, Marriott built two different hotels nearby. The first was on Main Street at 46th. It became the Holiday Inn Crowne Plaza when Marriott decided to spend millions to acquire land on 47th Street across from the Seville Square parking structure. That unit then became Sheraton Suites when Marriott took on the management of the Allis Plaza Hotel in downtown Kansas City. In the middle 1990s, the Plaza Inn was greatly remodeled into a Wyndam Hotel property. On top of the increase in hotel rooms, during the summer months and again in December each year, dozens of tour busses transport residents arriving from smaller communities all over Missouri and Kansas. They come to shop at the Plaza and Crown Center as well as to see other sites in the metro region.

What does all this mean for the Plaza that Kansas Citians know and love? It means that the store mix will continue to change in order to accomadate the changing needs of the customer. More boutiques and restaurants catering to the office worker clientele will likely move into spots vacated by shops whose merchandising concepts or style of operation contain less appeal for this new customer base.

Where at one time the Plaza largely existed by catering to the needs of immediate residents, successful retailers in the future will need to take the office work force into account. Most of the daily service-type stores that prevailed from the 1920s through the 1950s disappeared with the coming of Hall's and the expansion of Swanson's. Grocery stores, drug stores, dry cleaning establishments and others gradually sought space nearby but not on the Plaza itself. This resulted at least as much from the changing nature of those types of stores.

By contrast, persons frequenting the Plaza in the 1980s and '90s tended to come to eat, shop, stroll, and even to ride the horse-drawn carriages and buggies that operated from stands in front of Seville Square. Fewer customers came to buy basic products for house and home. Even those living in apartments or condominiums near the Plaza more frequently ate in restaurants than prepared meals at home.

Indeed, the growth in apartments and luxury condominiums ringing the Plaza provided the second major impact on Plaza shopping patterns in the 1980s and '90s. The 1920s witnessed the construction of such units

as the Locarno, the David Copperfield, the Walnuts, and a host of brick "three-story-walk-ups" along 47th Street. The Depression and World War II prevented apartment construction in the Plaza vicinity as they did elsewhere.

In the 1950s and '60s, taller structures such as Wornall Plaza, Regency House, the Sulgrave, the Winston Churchill, and others took their places as new residential units south and west of the Plaza. In the 1980s, the move was to high-rise luxury condominiums such as Alameda Towers, 433 Ward Parkway and Townsend Place. The first two buildings are located south of Brush Creek behind or just west of the Ritz-Carlton Hotel, respectively. Townsend Place went in on 46th Terrace immediately behind the old Macy's store now occupied by Barnes & Noble Booksellers, the Pottery Barn, and Canyon Café.

The Plaza area included slightly more than 6,000 apartment and condominium units within easy walking distance of its stores and restaurants in the mid-1990s. The vast majority of these were rented to comparatively young or middle-aged professionals, most frequently with all apartment occupants employed outside the home on a daily basis. Few families with children lived in any of the Plaza-area apartments. All these factors illustrate the marked change from the 1920s and '30s when significant numbers of families lived in Plaza-area apartments and from the 1960s and '70s when the apartments tended to contain larger numbers of older or retired residents.

Thus, the Plaza not only changes in its stores and attractions, the very customer base on which it must survive has changed substantially in recent years. The larger number who live and work in the immediate region serves to drive the types of stores and services desired and frequented on a regular basis.

Plaza Feature: Lighting the Plaza

The Plaza is justly famous for its Holiday lights. To be honest, they defy description. Photographs are necessary, but even then, it is impossible to capture the entire effect in one picture. The saying, "You have to be there," seems just about right for describing the scene. If one is fortunate enough to witness the Christmas lights reflected in new fallen snow, the term "winter wonderland" will do.

The holiday season comes to the Plaza on Thanksgiving night each year. On that night, 250,000 or more stand in the streets and sidewalks or on the hillsides in order to view the split second in which the reds, greens, blues, yellows, and whites all burst into brilliance at the same time. The lights stay lit until mid January of the following year.

The other ten and one-half months of the year, Plaza lights form a more subtle, yet very important aspect in developing the sense of its being a special place. The Giralda Tower is brightly lit at its base; the tower midsection is left in semi-darkness for effect. The open space that would be for the bells in the original is lighted in a bright white. The very top section above the bell openings shines in a contrasting yellow. The overall effect at a distance is breathtaking.

Not surprisingly, the other towers placed intermittently about the Plaza also serve as lighting focal points. In each instance, the bell sections are lighted from within, although none are as brightly lit as is the Giralda. The subtle earth tones and contrasting blues and deep greens appear even more inviting with the dimmed interior lighting effect.

Many of the buildings including the Mill Creek (Figlio), the Plaza Medical (Eddie Bauer), and the one sustaining the Giralda Tower (Cheesecake Factory and Mark Shale), are lit from under the eves. Light spreads from that high vantage point down over the rough brick and stucco exteriors, giving a palpable texture to the structures even more striking than in daylight.

Possibly the most arresting night view of the Plaza is the approach on 47th Street from the east. In a long unbroken line down the center of 47th stands the "Path of Gold" lights. These fixtures were molded from wooden patterns used in making lights for San Francisco's Path of Gold. Each standard features three globes high in the air emitting a golden yellow glow and individual bas-relief panels on the base. The Miller Nichols family presented this outstanding display to Kansas City in 1991.

Attention to detail is one of the hallmarks of the Plaza experience. Lighting is so important to establishing mood for evening shoppers, restaurant-goers and movie fans. In this, as in everything else, there is nothing quite like the Plaza at night!

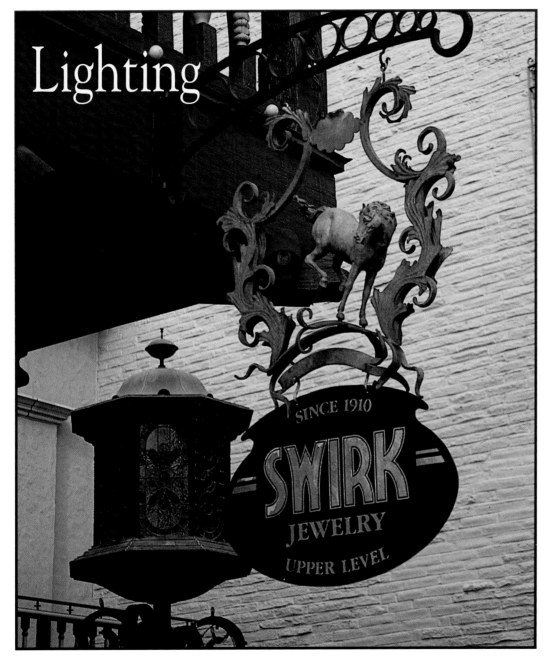

Lighting

SWIRK
SINCE 1910
JEWELRY
UPPER LEVEL

The phrase, "Plaza Lights," usually refers to the Christmas lights shining from Thanksgiving through mid January each holiday season. Just as exciting at other times, dramatic Plaza lighting creates a unique atmosphere at night.

Ornamental lamp to guide one's way along a Plaza path.

Streetlight [part of the Path of Gold] and wall light.

Detail of Path of Gold streetlight fixture, 47th St.

Ornamental light, Plaza Theater Building, Central St.

Stairway torch at Canyon Cafe, Broadway north of 47th St.

Under-the-eves lighting, Home Collection, Pomona Court, Broadway at Ward Parkway.

Store window treatment of shirts and ties, Brooks Brothers, Nichols Rd.

Store window lighting of folk art figures, Hall's, Nichols Rd.; Night lighting of signs at Hall's.

Carriage [red streaks] passing Jules' Seafood Restaurant, Jefferson at Nichols Rd.

Window treatment lighting, Pinstripes, 48th & Pennsylvania.

F. A. O. Scwartz is a favorite for both children and adults.

On this busy day the Plaza Art Fair was in full swing along Nichols Road.

Chapter 9:
Ever Changing ... for the Better

THE 1990S PROVED TO be almost as challenging to the Plaza's resilience as had the 1970s. During the latter decade, however, the crisis was internal to the management of the J.C. Nichols Company more than it was a change of outward direction. Part of the transition came from the natural flow of events surrounding the retirement of Miller Nichols in 1988. The biggest part of the challenge came from management decisions in the early '90s which placed continued Nichols Company management of the Plaza in jeopardy.

Miller Nichols achieved something with the Nichols Company and its crown jewel—the Plaza—which is little short of miraculous. He took over as president with the death of his almost legendary father in 1950 and improved on the work accomplished by J.C. Nichols. Rarely do entrepreneurial efforts so centered around one individual continue or expand once that person is no longer on the scene. Even more rarely do sons take over thriving businesses from their fathers and succeed to even greater degrees than did the original generation.

Miller Nichols constantly had to endure comparisons with J.C. Nichols throughout his tenure as president and chairman of the board (1950-1988).

"Do you think J.C. would have done it that way?"

"Boy, if J.C. were still alive, none of this would have happened!"

These were frequent comments over the decades.

The successful transition was not purely the work of Miller himself. J.C. Nichols placed tremendous trust in J.C. Taylor who guided the company as board chair for 13 years following Nichols' death. Treasurer Frank Grant continued to watch expenditures like a hawk until his death in 1960. J.C. Nichols' nephew, Ansel Mitchell, guided the construction department carefully through the wild days of the late 1940s and '50s.

Miller, Eleanor, and Clyde, the Nichols children, determined to leave Company profits largely invested in the Company rather than take them out in dividends or huge salaries. That does not mean that Miller was underpaid. It also does not mean that everyone else fully appreciated the low-dividend policy.

Cousin Ansel Mitchell, for example, became so exasperated with reinvested dividends that he sold or gave away enough shares of his stock to

A view of the Nelson-Atkins Museum of Art with Bruch Creek improvements in the foreground.

force the Company into "publicly held" status in the 1960s. For more than two decades, the Company had to publish public financial statements and allow glimpses by outsiders into what Miller clearly regarded as "family business." Finally, in the mid-1980s, Miller succeeded in repurchasing enough stock that he could take the Company back into private "closely held" status shortly before he retired.

In 1980, the Board of Directors elected former Treasurer Lynn McCarthy as President to succeed Davis K. Jackson. When Miller announced his retirement as Board Chair (but not from Board membership), McCarthy took on the title as Chairman of the Board as well.

Part of Miller's retirement from active leadership of the Company resulted in the sale of much of Nichols family-owned stock to the Company Employee Stock Benefit Plan. This Company-managed retirement for its employees did have millions of dollars in assets by this time, but it didn't really have sufficient assets to pay cash for the Nichols family stock. As a result, the Company had to sell some properties and mortgage others (including most of the Plaza).

By 1995, things were getting difficult due to heavy loan interest payments. During the effort to find outside sources of cash around 1990, the Nichols Company invited a New York investment banking business, Allen & Company, into the development of a projected upscale residential development in Johnson County. LionGate, with over 90 acres of prime residential sites, looked to be a sure way to generate future profits. Even with the Allen cash infusion, however, the Nichols Company decided not to proceed with LionGate at that time.

In order to placate the investment bankers, Lynn McCarthy exchanged stock in the Nichols Company for their share of the land deal. This gave

Allen & Company access to Company financial records. As 1992 turned into 1994, the New York investors grew increasingly concerned about the management of the Company. By 1995, they began suits to force Nichols management to alter its practices.

At first Mr. McCarthy chose to ignore Allen & Company's concerns. Instead, he concentrated on building support among his Board of Directors and in the community. He painted Allen & Company as "takeover artists" who were simply trying to gain control of the Nichols Company for as little cash as possible.

The Allen & Company suits generated action among a portion of the Board members including Miller Nichols. They empowered an attorney to investigate the charges against McCarthy and certain other Company officials brought by Allen & Company in its suits. Events came to a head in May 1995 when the Board of Directors relieved McCarthy of his responsibilities along with other officials in the Company closely tied to him. For a period of time, Jack Frost, took over as interim president.

Because the McCarthy episode seemed to reflect on the quality of the Board of Directors, there were several resignations followed by election of a new "community leader" Board which included such persons as the late Paul Henson of Kansas City Southern Industries and contractor William Dunn. This Board selected a new management team and permanent board members in 1996. The choice for president was a young man trained at J.E. Dunn Construction Company, E. Barrett Brady.

All this transition meant that the Nichols Company henceforth would be a publicly held company. Stockholders approved an 80-to-1 stock split in 1996 to reduce the price per share into a range where ordinary investors could afford to buy whenever they came on the open market.

Midwest Research Institute, Frank Theis Park and the William Volker Fountain all lie southeast of the Plaza along Brush Creek.

The importance of all this internal change in the Nichols Company to the present and future of the Plaza is more than academic. Most of the first 74 years of the Plaza's existence occurred while the J.C. Nichols Company operated as a closely held private company. Even during the period when the number of share holders was sufficient to require public financial reports, the primary leadership came from Miller Nichols and his handpicked leadership team.

Up to 1996, the Plaza evolved as the private property of a single family and a select group of employees. The transition to public ownership brings with it greater public accountability, but also a management style that necessarily brings more personalities into future decision-making about the shopping area and other Company properties. Because of the significant debt inherited from previous management decisions, this public company management team must be even more careful in the future to make decisions with an eye to the bottom line.

Clearly, as long as J.C. Nichols, and then Miller Nichols controlled the direction of the Plaza, profit-and-loss issues mattered, but other factors such as appearance, acceptance, and control mattered equally with money issues. Current and future Plaza managers may not have the luxury of making decisions that do not inherently show promise of increased profits in the short term.

The Nichols family philosophy of plowing profits back into Company

expansion rather than into shareholder dividend checks can no longer be followed. High interest payments and a public shareholder constituency require the Company to seek the most profitable approaches, first and foremost.

An examination of the most recent changes on the Plaza may help in sorting out the immediate impact of the management changeover. In 1996, two new store buildings went up on the west end of the parking station between 47th and Nichols Road, Central to Broadway. These stores opened in November as The Great Train Store and the KCPT Store of Knowledge.

Most substantial of all, plans for a huge Plaza expansion became public early in 1997. Brady and other Company executives announced proposed projects for retail, hotel, office, and apartment space. The improvements would be financed through a public-private partnership between Kansas City, Mo., and the J.C. Nichols Company. The Company planned to ask for Tax Increment Financing to target future tax revenues generated in the new properties to help construct the various parking improvements. Company planners included a total of $55 million in targeted tax revenues for this purpose. The total cost of all the proposed improvements came to $240 million.

The hope of the Company is that these changes will continue to make the Country Club Plaza the premier shopping area of the Kansas City Metropolitan Region into the 21st Century.

Plaza Profile: Barrett Brady

When the transition Nichols Board of Directors chose E. Barrett Brady as Nichols Company president in 1996, it selected a man with a pedigree for the job, if not the usual type of experience.

Barry Brady, as he is more frequently known, had a strong business background of almost 20 years with Dunn Construction. Additionally, his father, Fred Brady, served on the Nichols Company board in the 1950s and '60s. Fred Brady represented City Bond and Trust Company, an investment partner with the Nichols Company in the construction of Regency House and The Sulgrave apartment buildings in the 1960s. Beyond that, Barrett Brady's grandfather was none other than J.C. Taylor, J.C. Nichols' "right-hand man" and Nichols board chair from 1950 to 1963.

With the transition to public company status, Brady brought business and people skills to the position which would be sorely needed. The Nichols Company needed to pay off debt from the stock purchase of the late '80s, fight off increasing competition from suburban centers and increase its own opportunities for growth over the next decades.

It will be a different kind of J.C. Nichols Company that tackles the challenges of the new century. The land development company has evolved into a business management concern. While clearly engaged in aspects of the real estate business, the Nichols Company looks to the future in planning for increased management opportunities in newly constructed facilities around the Plaza as well as continuing the high level of quality it demonstrated over its first 75 years and more. Barrett Brady is in position to lead that effort forward.

Ever Changing ... for the Better

139

It could be 4:30 p.m. in any Mediterranean city from Spain to Morocco. It happens to be 4:30 in Kansas City on the Country Club Plaza. Welcome to America's first automobile suburb shopping center. Welcome to the center of evening restaurant life and shopping in the heart of metropolitan Kansas City.

Chapter 10:
Plaza Discovery Tour

It could be 5:00 in Chicago or New York or on the waterfront in any northern city in late winter. It happens to be in Kansas City. Welcome to cosmopolitan living adjacent to the Country Club Plaza.

At nighttime, the Plaza lights up in a million ways. From the downcast glare of light on the Brush Creek walkways to the brilliantly lit Plaza Time Tower, Plaza visitors find new views and intriguing places to explore day or night.

At Christmastime, the Plaza is glorious by day and night as well. Here we look west on 47th Street toward the Sheraton Suites Hotel. The "path of gold" lights are reminiscent of those in San Francisco, but the blend of architecture is pure Kansas City—at the Country Club Plaza, that is.

By now, the pattern is clear. The Country Club Plaza is a wonderful blend of urban excitement and architectural distinctiveness. Let's go on a Walking Tour of the Plaza. We'll see some things that even Plaza watchers with decades of experience might have missed. And, we'll see some of the newest buildings and art decoration to be seen.

First, let's focus on the buildings themselves. Of course, the overall effect is that of Mediterranean Spain or the South of France. We'll see bits of Mexico, South America, and North Africa along the way as well. Keep your eyes open for the little details that give the Plaza the extra appeal not found in any single part of the world mentioned.

Look up to see the towers that mark the Plaza skyline.

A central plaza in sunny Spain? While a distinct possibility, it's but a few steps from the Mediterranean bell tower and only a block from the scene of the high-rise luxury apartments in winter. As the seasons change on the Country Club Plaza, the vistas unfold in delightful variety.

Towers

One of the most visible features of the Plaza is the presence of numerous towers with wonderfully varied designs and touches. The first of these to catch one's attention is the Giralda Tower at 47th and J.C. Nichols Parkway.

Plaza area residents often see the Giralda Tower as simply the tallest and most ornate of the many tall Plaza towers spread throughout the shopping area. This is a common view from any number of high-rise apartment and condominium units surrounding the central shopping location.

The experienced Plaza aficianado will recognize this view of the Giralda from between the twin towers of Casa Loma apartments with the American Century office building as a backdrop. From this viewpoint, one begins to realize the true urban center that the Plaza has become.

Against the black night sky, the Giralda Tower takes on an even more magnificent appearance. The variation of lighting on the bell tower portion is nicely complemented by the under-the-eves lighting of the Cheesecake Factory at its base. The Tower tip stands out as a beacon for all.

As one focuses more closely on the tower, the detail of the Statue of Faith stands clear. It is this figure which gave the original Giralda Tower in Seville, Spain, its name. The statue was a weathervane which turned in the wind to indicate the prevailing gusts. In Spanish, "giralda" means "weathervane."

The bell tower of the Giralda at sunset calls to mind the purpose of the original tower in Spain. It called the faithful to worship, to mourn, and to celebrate at the various festivals of the city of Seville. An electronic carrillon in the Plaza Giralda provides both the tone of the hours and the delight of various recorded songs and anthems.

In order to fit with the more human scale of the Plaza as a whole, Nichols Company architects reduced the dimensions to one-half their original size in Spain. Had the Kansas City Tower been constructed at the same scale as the original, it would easily have been the tallest building in the city and dwarfed the one and two-story structures surrounding it.

Possibly the second-most photographed Plaza Tower anchors the entrance to the Plaza from the southern approach along Wornall Road. One place to view it at some distance is across the newly refurbished Brush Creek creekbed. Framed by an overhanging branch, this magnificently tiled tower draws the attention of motorists all along busy Ward Parkway.

Closer examination of Plaza Time brings its brilliant tilework into focus. The golden hues of the very top are produced by brightly shining ceramic rather than gold leaf or other metallic coating. The four clock faces provide a handy reference to shoppers in the central to west end sections of the Plaza area.

The morning sun brightly outlines the Plaza Time tower. Colorful tiles form geometric patterns on the lower sections of the structure as well as on the top dome.

Sunset provides possibly the most vivid view of the simple form of the Plaza Time Tower for Plaza residents and visitors alike.

The brilliant blue color of the small dome topping the Plaza Theater Tower provides another distinctive spot for Plaza visitors. This remarkable theater, constructed in the 1920s has had continuous use as a movie theater longer than any other theater in Kansas City. Additionally, it has served as a venue for the Kansas City Philharmonic and occasional stage plays and presentations.

The Plaza, First and Always

The Tower on the Tower Building. This was the first tower constructed on the Plaza. It dates from 1923 when the building went up as a compliment to the Wolferman Grocery Store. In the 40 years before the erection of the Giralda Tower across the street, this particular tower drew much of the attention of shoppers and visitors entering the Plaza District from the east.

Even in the 1990s, it remains an impressive creation as it reigns over art galleries and nearby restaurants.

Balcony Building Towers; the Plaza Welcome Tower, and Figlio's Tower.

The Balcony Building Towers are square structures appropriately featuring small balconies. These Plaza features went up in 1924-25.

By contrast, the Plaza Welcome and Figlio Towers are quite recent additions. The first was donated by the Miller Nichols family in an attempt to dress up the end of the rather plain Triangle Building [built in 1924]. This tower at 47th and Central gets its name from the welcome information activities carried on under its colorful dome.

The Figlio Tower with its resplendent copper accents appeared in the 1980s to draw attention to the northeast corner of the Plaza and the fine Italian restaurant which operates under it.

Domes

Equally impressive are the domed structures which punctuate the rooflines with rounded smoothness.

Dome at Parkway 600, Pennsylvania & Ward Parkway.

Modernist open dome above Commerce Motor Bank, 46th Terrace & Wyandotte; Dome above Barami's, Central & Nichols Rd.

Building Decoration

The surprise of delightful building decoration provides one of the truly enchanting aspects of a walk through the Plaza. To appreciate these features fully, it is necessary to walk while looking upward and inward to walls and roof lines. Needless to say, a walk to observe the building embellishments is best scheduled during an unhurried period such as an early summer's morn.

Building lentil decoration on the Mill Creek [Suydam] Building facing J.C. Nichols Parkway; Arcade across the ground level of the Pottery Barn. This feature recalls an earlier tenant of the building—Emery-Bird-Thayer Department Store—and the building that store occupied in Downtown Kansas City.

Window and tile work above the entrance to Country Club Bank on Nichols Rd. just west of Broadway; Scallop and face at roof line of the Balcony Building, north side of 47th, east of Broadway.

Window decoration atop the west wing of Casa Loma apartments, Ward Parkway at J.C. Nichols Parkway.

Ornate window treatment at the Locarno Apartments, 239 Ward Parkway; Column capital in the shape of a cherub's head on the Balcony Building.

Ornamental stonework above entrances to Mill Creek [Suydam] Building.

Exterior wall decoration, Balcony Building; Decorative iron work on second story of the J.C. Nichols Company Building, Ward Parkway.

Decorative nameplate for Harold's, 47th St.; Exterior of exit door from Plaza Theater, Nichols Rd.

Contrast of grillwork, signage, tiles, and awning, Houston's Restaurant, Wornall Rd.

Moorish-styled entrance to Hall's, Nichols Rd.

Figures set into exterior wall design, Seville Square [Sear's], Nichols Rd.; Entrance steps and roofline variation, The Great Train Store & The KCPT Store of Knowledge, Broadway.

Tile work under roof line of Helzberg's, Broadway at Nichols Rd.

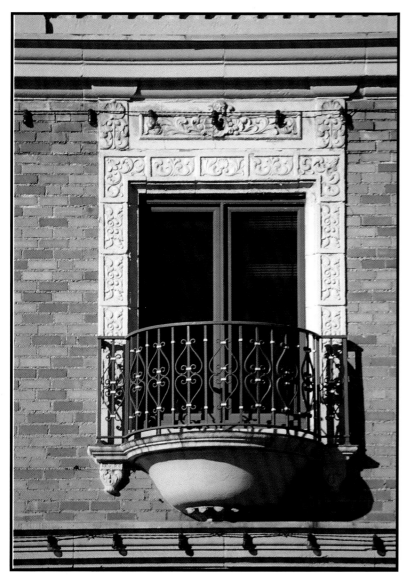 

Window treatment, including balcony, Plaza Theater Building, 47th St.; Finial above Pomona Court, Home Collection, Broadway at Ward Parkway.

Painted tile scene of Universidad Nacional de Mexico, alleyway off Pennsylvania behind Scandia Down; Painted tile scene, Broadway & Nichols Rd.

Brick design on exterior of Seville Square, Nichols Rd. & Pennsylvania; Grillwork and window treatment, Plaza Theater Building, Central St.

Tile work and window decoration, J.C. Nichols Company Building, Ward Parkway; English Tudor styled fronts of "Peanuts" Apartments, 49th & Central.

Window treatment and exterior wall design above the Nature Company, Broadway.

Saks signage and Plaza bench; Details of Plaza bench seat backs.

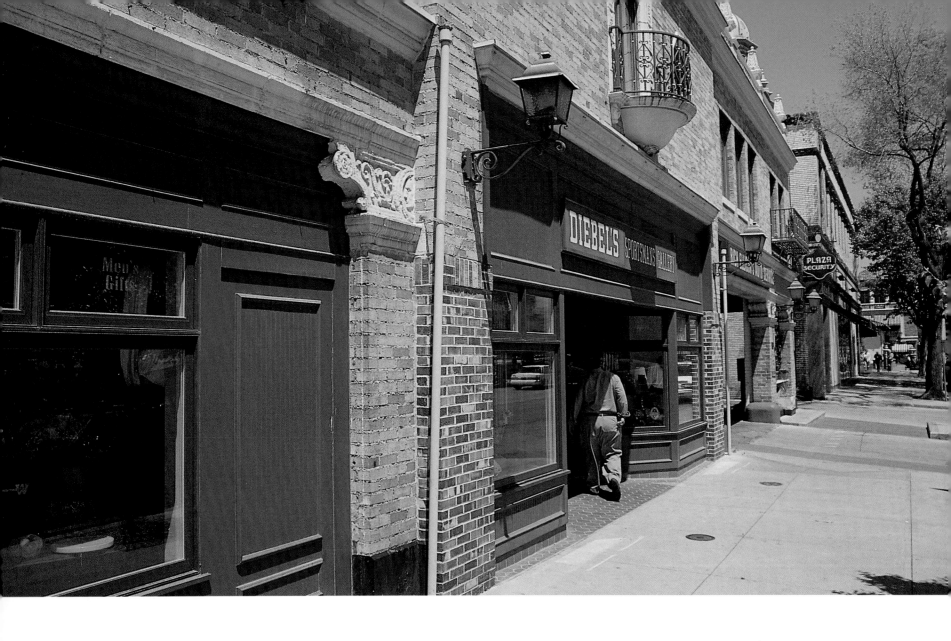

The Plaza, First and Always

Shepherd Fountain, Fountain Cafe, 47th & J.C. Nichols Parkway.

Facade, Three Dog Bakery, 48th St.;

Facades of stores in J.C. Nichols Company Building, Ward Parkway.

View through Court of the Penguins, Nichols Rd.

Bridge over Brush Creek.

Emile's European Deli & Restaurant, Central & Nichols Rd.; Stroll along 48th St.

Mermaid Fountain Court, Eddie Bauer, Broadway & Nichols Rd.

Shoppers meander along Ward Parkway in Springtime.

Bacchus Fountain in Winter, Chandler Court, Cheesecake Factory, 47th & Wyandotte.

Plaza area apartment, 900 Ward Parkway.

The Plaza, First and Always
186

Thus we come to the end our Plaza Discovery Tour. Actually, it is only the beginning. There are so many sights and details to see that shoppers and visitors can come back regularly and always see something they haven't noticed before.

Partly, this results from the constant change and updating which keeps the Plaza the premier shopping destination that it is.

Partly, it grows out of the fact that one can never see ALL of the Plaza at any one time. New excitement and visual delights await one on every visit. Come see for yourself the wonder of the Country Club Plaza in Kansas City!

The Plaza, First and Always
188

Afterward: A Salute to the Past and a Commitment to the Future

IN ORDER TO MAINTAIN the Country Club Plaza as Kansas City's premier shopping area, the J.C. Nichols Company faces the responsibility of fulfilling a public trust as well as a private goal of profitability. As has always been necessary, decision-makers evaluating Plaza tenants remain flexible while always balancing their goals with the need to stay familiar.

Across the United States, the Plaza is recognized as the first automobile-based shopping center in the country. Beyond that, within professional circles, it is also recognized as one of the most successful shopping areas in the country, period.

More importantly, in the Kansas City region and its adjacent territory, residents and shoppers express concern for the welfare of the Plaza on a regular basis. People look out for the little things. Not too long ago, a lady called the Plaza Merchants Association offices during the holiday season to report that one red bulb found its way into the array of white bulbs outlining the tower on the Plaza Time building above Williams-Sonoma. It is that kind of public interest in even the smallest of things that makes the Plaza unique.

For the newly reorganized J.C. Nichols Company leadership, this sense of "public ownership" of the Plaza has its positive and negative sides. On the plus side, it means that a wide variety of people from all over the metro area and beyond consider it, "their Plaza." This feeling exists without any need for an advertising campaign or publicity effort to generate it. It means that people regularly come to the Plaza to assess its current condition and to speculate about its future in the city and the region. All this is to the good.

The Country Club Plaza has always been changing, trying new possibilities, looking ahead to changing trends in retailing and in customer desires.

This volume is an attempt to explain how the Plaza is...First and Always. The former claim is a fact, now demonstrated, that J.C. Nichols, Edward Buehler Delk, Herbert Hare, Edward Tanner and George Tourtellot by 1922 created the first planned automobile shopping center in the United States. The latter claim is really a hope and a promise that the Plaza will continue to evolve as the premier shopping area of the city and region well past the beginning of the 21st Century.

No other large shopping district in the United States has lasted more than 75 years. Even large downtown shopping areas in most U.S. cities have undergone such transformation as to be unrecognizable in the instances where they continue to exist at all.

According to merchandising textbooks, shopping areas are supposed to contain anchors which will attract customers for other stores as well. In Kansas City, the Country Club Plaza is an anchor for the city as a whole. Thus, for the sake of Kansas City and its metropolitan region, the Country Club Plaza is, indeed, "First...and Always."

The Plaza, First and Always
190

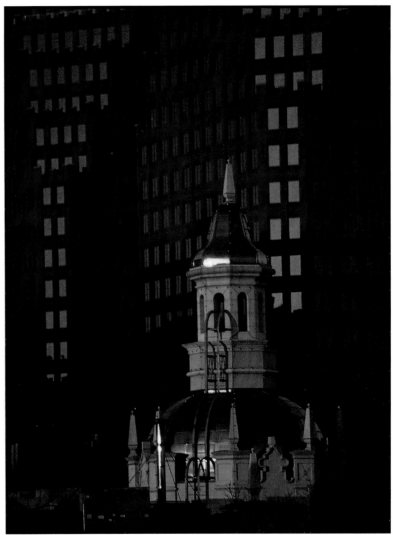

Lively little girl hugging Penguin Statue, Court of the Penguins, Pennsylvania & Nichols Rd.

Photography Credits

All Photography by Gary Carson except the following:

High View Aerial Photography 118, 132, 134, 136; Dale Lightfoot, Lightfoot Photography 2-3, 6-7, 14-15; The Ritz-Carlton Hotel, Kansas City 90; J.C. Nichols Company 18, 20, 21, 22, 24, 30, 32 (photo by Chris Wilborn), 36, 44, 45, 50, 56, 65, 70 (photo by Phillip D. Rush), 72 (photo by Paul S. Kivett), 74, 75 (photo by Bill Mott); University of Missouri - Kansas City, Western Historical Manuscript Collection 16, 19, 23, 26, 33, 34, 35, 37, 39, 42, 52, 53, 54, 55, 58, 60, 62, 64, 66, 68.